Problem Solver

WITHDRAWN

Kevin W. Boyd

ALPHA

A member of Penguin Group (USA) Inc.

ALPHA BOOKS

Published by the Penguin Group

Penguin Group (USA) Inc., 375 Hudson Street, New York, New York 10014, USA

Penguin Group (Canada), 90 Eglinton Avenue East, Suite 700, Toronto, Ontario M4P 2Y3, Canada (a division of Pearson Penguin Canada Inc.)

Penguin Books Ltd., 80 Strand, London WC2R 0RL, England

Penguin Ireland, 25 St. Stephen's Green, Dublin 2, Ireland (a division of Penguin Books Ltd.)

Penguin Group (Australia), 250 Camberwell Road, Camberwell, Victoria 3124, Australia (a division of Pearson Australia Group Pty. Ltd.)

Penguin Books India Pvt. Ltd., 11 Community Centre, Panchsheel Park, New Delhi—110 017, India

Penguin Group (NZ), 67 Apollo Drive, Rosedale, North Shore, Auckland 1311, New Zealand (a division of Pearson New Zealand Ltd.)

Penguin Books (South Africa) (Pty.) Ltd., 24 Sturdee Avenue, Rosebank, Johannesburg 2196, South Africa

Penguin Books Ltd., Registered Offices: 80 Strand, London WC2R 0RL, England

Copyright © 2009 by Kevin W. Boyd

International Standard Book Number: 978-1-59257-802-3
Library of Congress Catalog Card Number: 2008931263

11 10 09   8 7 6 5 4 3 2 1

Interpretation of the printing code: The rightmost number of the first series of numbers is the year of the book's printing; the rightmost number of the second series of numbers is the number of the book's printing. For example, a printing code of 09-1 shows that the first printing occurred in 2009.

Printed in the United States of America

Note: This publication contains the opinions and ideas of its author. It is intended to provide helpful and informative material on the subject matter covered. It is sold with the understanding that the author and publisher are not engaged in rendering professional services in the book. If the reader requires personal assistance or advice, a competent professional should be consulted.

The author and publisher specifically disclaim any responsibility for any liability, loss, or risk, personal or otherwise, which is incurred as a consequence, directly or indirectly, of the use and application of any of the contents of this book.

Trademarks: All terms mentioned in this book that are known to be or are suspected of being trademarks or service marks have been appropriately capitalized. Alpha Books and Penguin Group (USA) Inc. cannot attest to the accuracy of this information. Use of a term in this book should not be regarded as affecting the validity of any trademark or service mark.

Most Alpha books are available at special quantity discounts for bulk purchases for sales promotions, premiums, fund-raising, or educational use. Special books, or book excerpts, can also be created to fit specific needs.

For details, write: Special Markets, Alpha Books, 375 Hudson Street, New York, NY 10014.

Publisher: Marie Butler-Knight
Editorial Director: Mike Sanders
Senior Managing Editor: Billy Fields
Acquisitions Editor: Tom Stevens
Development Editor: Nancy D. Lewis
Production Editor: Kayla Dugger

Copy Editor: Jan Zoya
Cover & Book Designer: Kurt Owens
Indexer: Brad Herriman
Layout: Brian Massey
Proofreader: Laura Caddell

Contents

Chapter 1. eBay and PayPal Account Management 1

Chapter 2. Buying Basics 21

Chapter 3. Power Buying 37

Chapter 4. Selling Basics 45

Chapter 5. Advanced Selling 87

Chapter 6. International Selling 105

Chapter 7. General eBay Questions 111

Chapter 8. Photography 123

Chapter 9. Domestic Shipping 135

Chapter 10. International Shipping 163

Chapter 11. eBay Stores 171

Chapter 12. Product Sourcing 181

Chapter 13. Accounting and Financials 197

Chapter 14. Legalities and Liabilities 207

Appendix A. A Complete Order-Fulfillment Process 213

Appendix B. Resources 219

Index 225

Introduction

If you are an eBay seller and have not experienced problems or ever had any questions, then you are definitely an exception. The rest of us, from time to time, need an eBay rescue.

This book is filled with questions. More important, it is full of answers, multiple solutions, flowcharts, seller tools, resource lists, guidelines, techniques, and strategies that will be your eBay problem solvers.

My teaching and consulting schedule keeps me in contact with solution seekers. The answers to my students' and clients' best questions are the basis of this book. They range from common and simple to rare and complex and are questions that most eBay sellers eventually have. You may choose to read this book cover to cover or use the *SEE ALSO* entries to skip to the chapter and category for the specific question you have.

Dedication

My sincere thanks to my students who, in their searching for answers, have asked all the right questions. In return, I offer this book. No more guesswork; questions answered, problems solved.

Acknowledgments

My sincere thanks to the publisher and the creative and knowledge-able editors that made this book possible. A special thank you to Tom Stevens, Lissa McGrath, Kayla Dugger, Jan Zoya, and Nancy Lewis.

Trademarks

All terms mentioned in this book that are known to be or are suspected of being trademarks or service marks have been appropriately capital-ized. Alpha Books and Penguin Group (USA) Inc. cannot attest to the accuracy of this information. Use of a term in this book should not be regarded as affecting the validity of any trademark or service mark.

eBay and PayPal Account Management

Registering on eBay and PayPal is straightforward and relatively simple. However, you should perform a few steps in a certain order to minimize confusion. For example, most people register on eBay and then Pay-Pal. I suggest reversing that order. This way, you can set up your eBay account so your eBay fees will be automatically paid from your PayPal account. I have outlined the registration process in this chapter and also provided a flow chart to help you keep the steps in the right order.

The Registration Process

The following steps take you through the process of registration:

1. Open a new checking account specifically for your eBay business. This will keep your personal money separate from your eBay money. When April 15 (tax time) rolls around, you will be glad you did. If you are a member of a credit union, a second checking account is usually free. Several banks also offer free checking.

2. Open a new e-mail address strictly for your eBay business. For the same reason you don't want to mix your personal and business accounts, you don't want to mix personal and business e-mails. If you are paying for your e-mail addresses, usually your provider offers several accounts for your monthly rate. You may already have unused accounts.

3. PayPal is how your customers will pay for the items you sell on eBay. Therefore, you need to open a PayPal account. You will use your new checking account and e-mail address to open your PayPal account. I suggest you read the entire PayPal section (starting at queststion 1.19), first before you proceed.

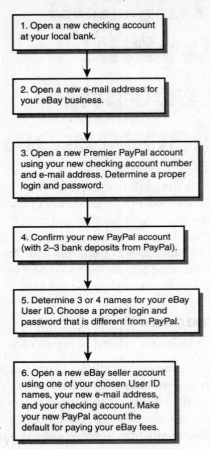

1. Open a new checking account at your local bank.

2. Open a new e-mail address for your eBay business.

3. Open a new Premier PayPal account using your new checking account number and e-mail address. Determine a proper login and password.

4. Confirm your new PayPal account (with 2–3 bank deposits from PayPal).

5. Determine 3 or 4 names for your eBay User ID. Choose a proper login and password that is different from PayPal.

6. Open a new eBay seller account using one of your chosen User ID names, your new e-mail address, and your checking account. Make your new PayPal account the default for paying your eBay fees.

eBay and PayPal Registration Flow Chart

To open a PayPal account, go to www.paypal.com and select the link to sign up for a new account. You will be given a choice of a Personal, Premier, or Business Account. As an eBay seller, you will want at least a Premier Account. This enables you to accept multiple forms of payments from your buyers with no limits to the number of transactions and at the best rate. See question 1.21 for an explanation of the three accounts.

You will need a suitable login and password. These should be different from any other account you have, including eBay.

This is very important in order to avoid hacker fraud. See question 1.1.

4. Confirm your new PayPal account. PayPal needs to confirm that your new checking account number is correct. They accomplish this by sending two small deposits to your account. You then need to verify the exact amount of their deposits. PayPal will send you an e-mail with instructions on how to accomplish this. See question 1.22.

5. Determine three or four names that you would like as an eBay User ID. You need more than one because there is a good chance that your first choice is already in use. I also suggest that you make the names generic rather than specific. This is because most sellers with a few months of experience usually are selling products that are quite different than the items they sold when they began. A generic name does not reflect any specific category and will not confuse your buyers as you change your products. See question 1.4.

6. Open an eBay seller account. Go to www.ebay.com and select the **Register** link to create a new account. Use your User ID(s), new e-mail address, and new checking account during account creation. When asked how you will pay your eBay fees, select PayPal and use your new PayPal account. Follow all directions and then don't forget to confirm your account when you receive the confirmation e-mail from eBay.

Logins, Passwords, and User IDs

1.1 "What is a good login and password?"

First, you must always use a different login or password for every significant online account you have. For example, your online bank, PayPal, and eBay accounts must each have a different login and password. The reason is identify theft. If a hacker or e-mail scammer could somehow trick you into revealing one login, they would have all your logins.

You should not use an actual word for a password. Instead, use a combination of at least six or more letters and numbers. Make the password easy for you to remember but difficult for anyone else to guess. For example, say you are a football fan and Brett Favre is your favorite player. Let's say you also play golf and your daughter was born in 2003. A good password then would be golf03favre. You can remember that but no one else could guess it.

1.2 "I signed up for eBay and PayPal a few years ago and forget my login information—what can I do?"

There are "I forgot my User ID" and "I forgot my password" links on eBay's sign-in page. Click the **Get help** link where it says "Having problems with signing in?" For the User ID, enter your e-mail address associated with the eBay account and it automatically e-mails you your User ID. For a password, enter your User ID and then it will e-mail you your password. If you are still having problems, see if a live eBay or PayPal representative can help you. For a live eBay rep, go to www.ebay.com and click on the **Live help** link near the top right of the screen. This will open a live chat window with an eBay representative. Be patient: if the traffic volume is high, it may take a few minutes for the representative's response. Once he is online, type your problem and see if he can help you. He will ask you some security questions that you had originally created when you signed in. Most likely, you will be able to answer his questions and he will give you a new, temporary password to get you going again.

For forgotten PayPal passwords, go to www.paypal.com and select the **password** link under the login button. Enter the e-mail address you used for account creation and follow all instructions from there. For forgotten e-mail addresses, select the **e-mail address** link.

If all else fails, call their customer service number 402-935-2050. PayPal customer service agents are available to help you during the following times: 4:00 A.M. PST to 10:00 P.M. PST Monday through Friday; 6:00 A.M. PST to 8:00 P.M. PST on Saturday and Sunday.

1.3 "Is it safe to give my checking account and routing numbers to eBay or PayPal?"

This information is printed clearly on your checks. Every business or individual you write a check to will have this information. I would trust reputable companies such as eBay and PayPal considerably more than I would a stranger.

1.4 "How can I determine a good User ID?"

Your User ID (username) will be the unique identifier of your eBay business. The name you choose will be a direct reflection as well as the first impression buyers will have of you. Avoid cute, silly, or weird names. Instead, create one that denotes professionalism. Again, I suggest that you create a generic name rather than something specific to the products you want to sell.

EBay has some limitations on User IDs. They cannot be, or contain, an e-mail or web address. They also must not contain spaces or symbols such as #, @, *, &, or contain the name eBay. Spend some time looking at the User IDs of the top sellers in the areas that you want to sell. Study their names to understand what a good username should be.

1.5 "How can I change my eBay User ID, password, e-mail address, checking information, or credit card information?"

You can easily change any of your personal information from your My eBay page.

1. Login to eBay and click on your **My eBay** tab.

2. Scroll down the left column until you see the My Account section. Click the **Personal Information** link.

3. This opens the page with all your personal information. You can now go to the proper section and edit your information for:

   E-mail and Contact Information

   User ID and Password

   Financial Information

1.6 "If I change my User ID (username), does my feedback follow me?"

Yes. Actually, your feedback remains and is linked to your new name.

1.7 "What if I have negative feedback and I don't want it to follow me?"

You don't have a choice, as this is automatic. Note that eBay removes negative and neutral feedback from your percentage score after one year. It will, however, still remain visible in your Feedback Profile. If the feedback was recent and you don't want to wait that long, or if you only have a few feedbacks in your account anyway, you may want to open a new account and start fresh. You would have a clean slate but zero feedback. See the next question.

1.8 "Can a user who has bad feedback open a new account to start over?"

Yes, but only if his original account was not suspended due to account issues or a serious eBay policy violation. EBay has software that looks for this type of activity. If a suspended user is found doing this to clean his slate, eBay will take appropriate action based on the severity of the problem in his original account.

To open a new account, you will need a different e-mail address and a different credit card.

1.9 "How often can I change my User ID?"

Every 30 days. But don't make a habit of it. EBay frowns on constant name changes and it confuses your customers. Also, after you change your name, a new icon will appear next to your User ID for 30 days to indicate that you changed your name. It is a bit of a red flag and some buyers may choose not to trade with you.

1.10 "What is ID Verify?"

ID Verify simply means that eBay has used a credit bureau to verify your identity. EBay uses your demographic information that you registered on eBay, along with specific questions that only you would know. The questions are similar to a loan application such as your monthly mortgage payment, the address of your last residence, car loan payments, and so on. This information is then sent to a credit bureau (Equifax in the United States) for verification. If the details match, you are verified.

The primary advantage of becoming ID Verified is providing instant credibility for a new account with zero feedback. You can also bid on items over $15,000. There is a $5 application fee for this service which is charged to your eBay account. You receive an icon next to your User ID to clearly show your buyers that you are ID Verified. You remain ID Verified until you change your registered address or phone number. After that, you need to follow the ID Verify process again (and pay the $5 fee again).

eBay Account Management

1.11 "How can I upgrade my buyer account to seller?"

If you already have a buyer account, then you can easily upgrade your account to seller. First, login to your eBay account. Then at the very top of the page, click the **Sell** link in the primary toolbar. EBay will ask if you want to "Create a Seller Account." Follow the instructions from there.

1.12 "How many eBay accounts can I have?"

As many as you want, provided each is registered with a separate User ID, e-mail address, and credit card.

1.13 "Should I have an account for eBay buying and a separate one for selling?"

It is your decision. Keep in mind that all feedback counts toward your total score whether it was received because of a purchase or a sale. Therefore, buying and selling all your items with the same User ID will help you gain feedback more quickly. You cannot receive neutral or negative feedback for a transaction where you were the buyer, so any buyer feedback you receive will positively increase your Feedback Score.

Separate accounts are not necessary unless you don't want your customers to see what you are purchasing. For example, if you are buying merchandise in "lots" on eBay and reselling the items individually, it would be best to keep those purchases separate and out of view, under another User ID.

1.14 "Can I have an eBay account and my spouse also have another one?"

Yes, you can have as many eBay accounts as you want as long as they all have a different User ID and e-mail address. The problem is not usually with multiple eBay accounts but with multiple PayPal accounts when both spouses try to use the same credit card for both accounts.

SEE ALSO **1.20** "Can I have a PayPal account and my spouse also have another one?"

1.15 "My account was suspended by eBay. What happened?"

EBay will notify you of a suspended account with an e-mail and also in the **My Message** link within your My eBay page. The message will explain why the account was suspended. An eBay account is usually suspended when the user has either ...

- Violated one of eBay's Rules and Policies.
- Not paid her monthly eBay fees.
- Received three separate Unpaid Item (UPI) strikes.

POWERSELLER TIP

A member with a suspended account cannot buy, sell, or leave feedback. This applies not only to his suspended account, but any other accounts that he may have. These members, his family members, and even his eBay business partners cannot open a new account. To learn more, choose the **Help** link and type **suspended account** in the search box.

1.16 "How can I get a suspended account reactivated?"

When you correct the reason for account suspension, your account will most likely be reactivated automatically. For example, often a suspension from lack of payment of eBay fees is simply because the credit card used to pay the fees has expired. When you provide eBay with the new credit card information, your account is reactivated.

Accounts that were suspended due to three UPI strikes can possibly be reactivated through an appeals process. If you feel your account was suspended due to error, you can appeal your case to eBay's Trust & Safety Team by filling out the proper web form. The case will then be reviewed and the decision made. To learn more, select the **Help** link, type **suspended account**, select **Reinstating Your Account,** and then **Contact Us** (at the bottom of the page).

1.17 "I keep getting these weird e-mails from eBay or PayPal claiming there is some problem with my account. What is going on?"

In almost every case these are bogus e-mails, called spoof or phishing e-mails. They are generated by criminals who want you to click on the link in the e-mail, which will take you to their spoof website. Their site looks very much like eBay or PayPal but they are nothing more than a phony storefront. They want you to believe you are on eBay or PayPal so you will enter your login and password. Once you do, you have given the keys to the criminals and they can hijack your account.

Never click on the link in these e-mails or enter your User ID and password. Ignore, delete, or, even better, report spoof e-mails to spoof@ebay.com.

1.18 "How can I tell the difference between a legitimate eBay or PayPal e-mail and a spoof e-mail?"

Use the following, along with the spoof e-mail flow chart, to help determine legitimate e-mails:

- Check the greeting. If it is addressed as "Dear eBay Customer (or member)," it is a spoof. The sender doesn't even know your name or User ID. Legitimate e-mails will greet you with both your first and last name, or your registered username.

- When an e-mail states that you must take immediate action or your account will be suspended, or that eBay is updating their files and wants to be sure your information is up to date, it is a spoof.

- If the e-mail asks for personal information such as login, password, or financial information, it is a spoof.

Spoof vs. Legitimate eBay and PayPal E-Mails

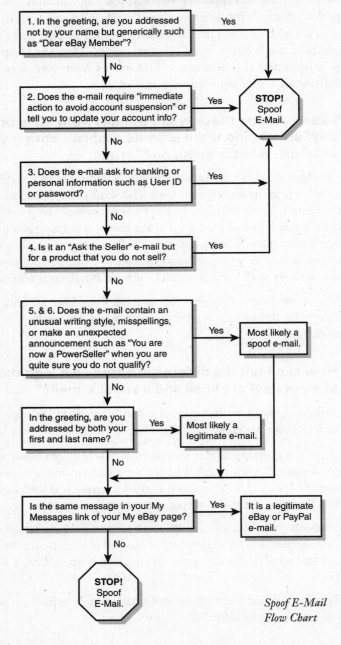

1. In the greeting, are you addressed not by your name but generically such as "Dear eBay Member"? — Yes →

2. Does the e-mail require "immediate action to avoid account suspension" or tell you to update your account info? — Yes →

3. Does the e-mail ask for banking or personal information such as User ID or password? — Yes →

4. Is it an "Ask the Seller" e-mail but for a product that you do not sell? — Yes →

STOP! Spoof E-Mail.

5. & 6. Does the e-mail contain an unusual writing style, misspellings, or make an unexpected announcement such as "You are now a PowerSeller" when you are quite sure you do not qualify? — Yes → Most likely a spoof e-mail.

In the greeting, are you addressed by both your first and last name? — Yes → Most likely a legitimate e-mail.

Is the same message in your My Messages link of your My eBay page? — Yes → It is a legitimate eBay or PayPal e-mail.

No ↓

STOP! Spoof E-Mail.

Spoof E-Mail Flow Chart

- If the e-mail looks like a legitimate "Ask the Seller" question from a buyer, look closely at the item for sale. If the item is not one of your listings, it is a spoof.

- Other spoof e-mails may contain misspellings, a poor writing style, or an unusually formatted e-mail.

- Any unexpected or undeserved claim such as "You are now a PowerSeller" is almost guaranteed to be a spoof.

Note that there are some exceptions to these rules. If an e-mail requires you to use the link provided within the e-mail to login to eBay or PayPal, it is most likely a spoof. However, PayPal will send you e-mails that have links to their site when you have been paid for an item. These e-mails contain links and do not normally show up in your **My Messages** link. These types of e-mails fall outside of these tests.

SEE ALSO **5.27** "What is the eBay Toolbar?"

Legitimate and important eBay and PayPal e-mail messages such as account problems or Second Chance Offers will always be available for review in your My eBay page under the **My Messages** link. If you think that an e-mail is legitimate, go directly to eBay and login to your account (do not click on the link in the e-mail). Check your **My Messages** link to see if the same message is there.

If you truly have a problem with your account such as suspension, you will notice it as soon as you attempt to login to your account. A message (called an alert) will appear stating that your account is suspended, and there will be instructions how to remedy the problem.

PayPal Account Management

1.19 "How can I change my account information on PayPal?"

You can change any of your personal information on PayPal using these steps:

1. Login to PayPal and click on your **My Account** tab.
2. In the upper right-hand corner, click on **Profile**.

3. This opens a page where you can edit all your account, financial, and selling preferences information.

4. Select the **Add** button to add the new change. Then make the new change **Primary** and select the **Confirm** button.

1.20 "Can I have a PayPal account and my spouse also have another one?"

Yes, you can as long as you both use different e-mail addresses, credit cards, and bank accounts for your accounts. The rule is that only one credit card or bank account can be used for one account and it must be unique to that account. Additionally, you can have one Personal Account and one Premier or Business Account. You cannot have two Personal, Premier, or Business Accounts assigned to one person. Finally, you can have eight separate subaccounts under one primary account.

Note that you do not need a different PayPal account for each eBay account. All of your eBay accounts can be linked to just one PayPal account.

POWERSELLER TIP

If you are considering opening several PayPal accounts, the rules can be a bit confusing. I suggest you contact PayPal for further information before you attempt opening multiple PayPal accounts.

1.21 "What is the difference between a Personal, Premier, and Business Account?"

Most buyers have a Personal Account that they use to pay for items purchased online. Although you can use a Personal Account to receive payments, your number of annual transactions is limited and the fees are high. Premier and Business Accounts are used by Internet and eBay sellers.

EBay sellers should have a PayPal Premier Account in order to accept unlimited numbers of all forms of payments, including credit cards, debit cards, and eChecks. The Premier Account also offers premium services such as access to interest from a high-yield money market fund, optional debit card, auction and website tools, and access to their customer call center. Most eBay sellers have a Premier Account.

Business Accounts are the best choice when a seller needs two or more logins and security levels. For example, maybe your employees need access to shipping addresses from your business PayPal account. However, you don't want them to have access to financial information or the ability to withdraw money.

1.22 "I just received an e-mail that says I have to confirm my new PayPal account. What is this and how do I do it?"

PayPal wants to be sure that the bank account and routing number you used to open your PayPal account are indeed correct. To accomplish this, they use an Instant Bank or Random Deposit process and send two or three small deposits (just a few cents) electronically to your bank account. You need to wait about two or three business days for the money to post to your account. To determine if it has posted, either call your bank or view your bank account online to see the deposits.

Once you have received the small deposits:

1. Login to your PayPal account.

2. Click the **Confirm Bank Account** link on your Account Overview page.

3. Enter the two or three amounts that PayPal deposited.

If the amounts are correct, your bank account is confirmed and your new account is activated. Note that this is not the same as a Confirmed address. See question 1.31.

Remember that this is all done for your safety. After you sell a few items on eBay, your PayPal account balance will grow. You will eventually need to electronically transfer some of that money from your PayPal account to your local bank account. You are now certain that it is going to be deposited into the correct account.

When paying for items using PayPal, if there are not enough funds in your PayPal account, the transaction defaults to an "Instant Payment

Transfer." PayPal will draw the funds from your bank account (first) or, if not enough funds are in the bank account, it will use the credit card you have on file. This is why I recommend registering both a bank account and credit card when setting up your account.

1.23 "What does a Verified account mean?"

To become a Verified account, a PayPal member must provide proof of an account at a bank or other financial institution. You can become verified when using the process described in question 1.22, or if during the registration process you were approved for a PayPal Buyer Credit or a PayPal Plus credit card. Because these institutions are required by law to screen account holders, PayPal's verification process lowers your risk when dealing with a Verified member as either a buyer or seller.

1.24 "Can I earn interest on my PayPal account?"

Yes, as long as you have a Premier or Business Account. The other good news is that their rates are usually comparable to a bank's CD rate.

1. Login to your Premier or Business PayPal account.
2. Select the **My Account** tab, then select **Overview.**
3. Under your balance will be a link called **Earn a return on your balance.** Follow the instructions from there.

Note that the interest earned will be reported to the IRS, so they will ask for your Social Security number.

1.25 "Can I deposit money in my PayPal account?"

Yes, you can add funds by transferring money from your bank account.

1. Login to your account and select the **Account** tab then select **Add funds.**
2. Now select the link **Transfer Funds from a Bank Account in the United States.**

Note that there is no PayPal fee to do this. Check with your bank first to see if they charge a fee for this service. Remember that if your PayPal balance gets too low and you purchase an item that is over your available funds, PayPal will default to an Instant Payment Transfer.

SEE ALSO **1.28** "If I have no money in my PayPal account, how can I pay for items on eBay?"

1.26 "How do I get money out of my PayPal account?"

You can withdraw money from your PayPal account in any of three ways:

ATM: If you have a PayPal debit card, you can use it to withdraw money up to $400 a day at any ATM machine that displays the Cirrus/Maestro logo. PayPal charges a $1 fee for this service. The ATM may also charge a fee.

Request a Check: You can request that a check be sent to you.

Online Transfer to a Credit Card or Bank Account: You can request that the money is transferred to either a credit card or to the bank account that you used when setting up your account (this is how I withdraw money). It will take about three or four days for the money to post to your account. You can also add a new checking account or credit card at any time for this purpose. To request an online transfer, use the **Withdraw** tab and follow the instructions.

1.27 "Are there limits to the payments I can make with PayPal?"

For security purposes, PayPal limits the amount you can purchase for a single transaction to $10,000. You will also have a daily limit when using your PayPal debit card. To see the spending limits on your particular account, select the **Account Overview** page and click the **View Limits** link. If you need to make a payment for an item over $10,000, I suggest you use an escrow service. EBay recommends www.escrow.com.

1.28 "If I have no money in my PayPal account, how can I pay for items on eBay?"

PayPal will use a Payment Transfer to withdraw the money from either the bank account or credit card you used to set up your PayPal account. If you have both a credit card and bank account on file, the funds will be withdrawn from your bank account as the default. You can, however, choose to change it to your credit card for that purchase if you wish.

Note that if you do this, the seller will receive a notice that you paid by eCheck. They may choose to wait to ship your item until they receive a second notice that the funds have cleared.

SEE ALSO   1.35 "What is an eCheck?"

Other PayPal Questions

1.29   "What are the fees associated with using PayPal?"

There are no fees to open any PayPal account and no fees to send money, transfer money to, or withdraw money from your account. The fees are only applied when you receive payments.

For Premier or Business Accounts, the fees vary between 1.9 and 2.9 percent plus 30 cents per transaction. Your particular rate will be based on sales volume. Fees for converting international payments vary between 2.9 and 3.9 percent plus 30 cents.

1.30   "The status of a payment I have received in PayPal says 'unclaimed.' What does that mean?"

It means that you have unclaimed money that was sent to you and is waiting for you to claim it. Most likely, you cannot claim it because your account cannot accept the form of payment made.

Many times it is because your PayPal account is a Personal Account and not a Premier or Business Account, and you received a credit card payment that has exceeded your annual limit (five). You can pay for items with a Personal Account, but you really need to have a Premier or Business Account to accept unlimited credit card payments from other members. Login to your PayPal account and upgrade your Personal Account to Premier or Business. See question 1.21 for a comparison of the accounts.

1.31   "What is a Confirmed address?"

PayPal confirms addresses when the account member's address registered on PayPal matches her credit card billing address. Buyers must have Confirmed addresses in order for the seller to qualify for Seller Protection. (PowerSellers do not have to meet this qualification.) Note that a Confirmed address is not the same as confirming a new PayPal account (see question 1.22).

1.32   "I've heard that PayPal is not as secure for purchases as a credit card. Is that true?"

There are some horror stories floating around about eBay and PayPal. Most are urban myths or a story that has been overblown by an angry buyer or seller. However, there are times when a fraudulent dispute will arise between buyer and seller. PayPal offers excellent protection programs for both buyers and sellers. You need to be aware of how to use the protection programs so both your purchases and sales qualify for the protection. See questions 1.33 and 1.34.

1.33   "What is PayPal's Buyer Protection Program?"

PayPal offers a Buyer Protection Policy to help eBay buyers recover payments from sellers for nondelivery or description fraud. A seller who qualifies for Buyer Protection is highly preferred over one who does not.

Note that the item in question must be tangible and not a service, e-book, or items that are e-mailed or downloaded. You must also file your claim within 45 days of the PayPal payment date.

You must also have paid for the item in a standard way by either using the **Pay Now** button, or using the **Send Money** tab in PayPal and selecting **pay for eBay items** and then entering your User ID and the Item number for the auction. You also must have paid all in one payment.

A seller automatically qualifies for the Buyer Protection Program when she meets the following requirements.

- Feedback Score of 50 or more
- A positive feedback percentage of 98 or better
- Verified member of PayPal
- Premier or Business PayPal account in good standing

When a seller offers Buyer Protection, it will be posted in her listings under the **Buy safely** section directly under **Meet the Seller.** You can also see if the seller offers buyer protection toward the bottom of her listing under the **Payment details** section.

Payments for items that qualify are protected with no limit for the item price and shipping. Click the **See eligibility** link in their **Buy safely** section to learn more about a particular seller. For more information on the PayPal Buyer Protection Program, click the **Help** link on eBay and type **PayPal buyer protection,** or on PayPal, go to https://www.paypal-promo.com/protection/terms.

1.34 "What is PayPal's Seller Protection Program?"

For sellers, PayPal is actually easier and safer than accepting credit cards directly from the customer to a merchant account. If you have a merchant account and your customer pays by credit card, he can claim you never shipped the item and then ask for a refund from his credit card company. Unfortunately, the credit card company will comply with the cardholder and not the merchant. They will refund his money, send you a chargeback, and then you are without the money and the merchandise.

With the Seller Protection Program, PayPal acts as the liaison between you and the credit card company. You can use this policy to protect yourself against fraudulent claims of nonshipment or when payment is made with stolen credit card numbers.

If a buyer files a dispute against you, PayPal's Resolution Center team becomes involved to help you resolve the dispute, free of charge. If the dispute resolution fails and the buyer files a fraudulent chargeback claim with his credit card company, PayPal will work along with you to fight it.

For further details on Seller Protection, select the **Help** link on eBay and type **PayPal Seller Protection.** On PayPal, go to https://www.paypal-promo.com/protection/terms.

1.35 "What is an eCheck?"

An eCheck is similar to writing a check, but it is handled by funds being transferred electronically from a buyer's bank account to the seller's PayPal account. It usually takes about four business days for the transaction to clear (but sometimes up to two weeks), so if you receive an eCheck, don't ship the item until you receive the follow-up e-mail from PayPal stating the payment has cleared.

Most buyers do not know this and assume that the money is sent immediately. Additionally, buyers who do not have a Verified PayPal account do not qualify for Instant Payment Transfers from their bank. If the funds in their PayPal account are too low to cover the purchase, PayPal withdraws the money from their bank account and it is treated as an eCheck. The buyer probably doesn't even know she has sent an eCheck, assumes you have been paid, and so she is expecting shipment immediately.

POWERSELLER TIP

When I receive an eCheck notification, I always send an e-mail to the buyer, notifying her that she has sent an eCheck so it will take a few business days to clear (up to two weeks) and then the item will be shipped. Note that the buyer can cancel her payment (or you can reject it) and she can resend the payment specifying her credit card as the funding source if time is of the essence.

1.36 "Can I use PayPal to pay for items that are not related to any eBay sale?"

Yes, I do this all the time. PayPal is not just for eBay transactions. You can pay for any item you buy, or send money to an individual or business, using the **Send Money** tab in your PayPal account. You can also request money from someone by sending an invoice with the **Request Money** tab. All you need is your trading partner's PayPal e-mail address.

Note that a Personal Account does have a monthly limit of $500. If you are sending more than $500, the recipient will need to upgrade to a Premier or Business Account.

1.37 "Is the money in my PayPal account FDIC-insured?"

PayPal uses FDIC pass-through insurance. This means that PayPal deposits the money in your PayPal account into FDIC-insured banks. Therefore your money is guaranteed up to $100,000. However, you are not earning interest on that money. It is similar to a non-interest-bearing checking or debit account.

If you choose to earn interest on your account, then your money will not be placed in FDIC banks but in a money market mutual fund. You will be earning interest but lose the FDIC protection. This is the same method that financial investment firms use.

SEE ALSO 1.24 "Can I earn interest on my PayPal account?"

1.38 "Because my PayPal money is either invested in an FDIC bank or money market mutual fund, does that mean I have to wait to get the money out of my account?"

No. This does not cause a delay in the withdrawal process that was detailed in question 1.26.

Buying Basics

It may seem that buying on eBay is as simple as shopping in a store, selecting something, paying, and leaving. However, there is an art and even a science to eBay shopping in order to find the best deals and beat your competition consistently.

This chapter addresses the most common questions and problems that eBay buyers encounter. It will also provide you with the test to determine whether a seller is credible and then the strategies to win the auction. We will begin with basic buying questions and then move into the questions and problems associated with power buying in the next chapter.

Communication and Feedback

2.1 "How can I contact the seller to ask him a question?"

In the upper right-hand corner of the listing under "Meet the Seller," select the link **Ask seller a question.** A web-form e-mail page will appear for you to enter your question. Note that you will need to login to your account first. You will also need to enter the eBay-provided security code that appears slightly distorted. This is required to protect the seller from unscrupulous e-mail spammers.

Once you submit your question, it will be delivered using eBay's pass-through e-mail service. EBay also uses an e-mail masking system where the seller will receive a "forward" address rather than your actual e-mail address. The seller will respond using the same method. This pass-through e-mail masking service is provided to protect both trading partners from unwanted spam e-mail from other members. In addition, many individuals use spam filters, and an e-mail from eBay will pass the filter and guarantee delivery where one sent directly to an e-mail address will not.

2.2   "How do I leave Feedback?"

Feedback is the way eBay members self-police the site. Both the buyer and seller can leave feedback comments and a score for their trading partner based on their experience with a particular transaction. It is expected that every sale on eBay will have a comment and rating from both the buyer and seller about the quality of the transaction.

Buyers can leave feedback for their seller up to 60 days after the listing ends. To leave feedback, click on the **Feedback** link under the My Account section of your My eBay page. Then choose the **Leave Feedback** link.

Note that sellers cannot leave a negative or neutral feedback rating for a buyer. However, this does not excuse buyers from fulfilling their payment obligation. Sellers can still leave negative comments and report nonpaying bidders who will then receive an Unpaid Item (UPI) strike. After three strikes, eBay will suspend the buyer's account.

SEE ALSO   **1.15 "My account was suspended on eBay. What happened?"**

SEE ALSO   **1.16 "How can I get a suspended account reactivated?"**

Buyers should always check the Feedback Profile of a potential seller before they bid. This will help them determine if the seller has a good profile or if previous buyers have reported particular problems through their ratings and comments.

You can view your Feedback Profile by clicking on the Feedback Score (the number in parentheses) next to your User ID. You can view other members' Feedback Scores by also clicking on the Feedback Score next to their User ID.

2.3   "Can I contact the bidders of an item to warn them about a seller, tell them the item is counterfeit, or where to get that item for less money?"

Absolutely not. This is called auction interference, and it can get you in trouble. If you persist in doing this, eBay will suspend your account. This is one of those times where you have to mind your own business. You should post appropriate feedback for the seller based on your transaction experience and hope that other potential buyers do their research and read the feedback comments.

Selling Formats

2.4 "What is a Buy It Now price?"

Sellers may choose to offer a Buy It Now (BIN) price for their item. This places a **Buy It Now** button on their listing with a stated price. If you select the button, the listing ends immediately and you win the item for the BIN price.

2.5 "What happened to the Buy It Now price? It has disappeared since I viewed the item yesterday."

If a seller offers a **Buy It Now** (BIN) button along with a **Place Bid** button, you have the choice of either placing a bid on the item or buying it immediately. If a buyer chooses to BIN, she wins the item. However, if a buyer places a bid instead, the listing converts to Auction-Style format, and so the BIN option is no longer available and the BIN button disappears. Therefore, the first bidder who enters the auction will determine which way it will go.

2.6 "Sometimes I see bids occurring and the Buy It Now button is still available. Why didn't it disappear?"

The seller is probably offering a reserve price with the same listing. The **Buy It Now** button will remain until the reserve price is met.

Note that items in certain categories can have their BIN option still available until bidding reaches 50 percent of the BIN price. Currently these categories include PDAs, cell phones, shoes, clothing, tickets, and the parts and accessories category on eBay Motors. Other categories may be added to this exception list in the future.

2.7 "What is a reserve price?"

A reserve price is the minimum price that a seller is willing to accept for an item. It is sometimes used to protect the seller from an expensive item being sold for too low a price. An auction that ends without the reserve price being met is considered a no-sale by eBay. The high bidder did not win and the seller does not have to part with the item.

Listings that have reserve prices have the link **Reserve not met** posted directly under the item's current price. A listing that has a reserve price that has already been met will display the **Reserve met** link. The reserve price is private between eBay and the seller. It is the seller's choice whether to reveal the reserve price in the listing.

2.8 "Is it okay to ask the seller what the reserve price is?"

Yes. E-mail the seller and ask him what the reserve price is for the item. He may or may not provide you with that information. There is nothing sneaky about a hidden reserve price. Most professional sellers do not reveal their reserves.

2.9 "What does a Best Offer listing mean?"

A Best Offer listing enables buyers to make an offer on the item much like an "Or Best Offer" (OBO) listing in a newspaper. It is similar to an Auction-Style format except the buyer submits his best offer instead of placing a bid. Sellers can choose to accept or decline the offer or make a counteroffer.

You will see a **Buy It Now** button and a **Best Offer** button. Most sellers who list a Best Offer expect to sell the item for less than the Buy It Now price, so always make an offer rather than clicking the **Buy It Now** button if you want that item.

2.10 "What are eBay Stores?"

An eBay Store is similar to having a website on eBay. Sellers use eBay Stores to list accessories, add-ons, or different items. Listings created exclusively for an eBay Store are always Buy It Now listings (also known as "Fixed Price listings").

Note that store listings do not appear in a standard keyword search unless the search produces less than 30 results. Usually you will find the seller's store by clicking on the store link within her listing. You can search exclusively for store items by using the **Advanced Search** link and then selecting **Items in Stores.** You can also click on the **Stores** tab from the homepage and then use the search box on that page that will only search store listings.

2.11 "What is eBay Express!?"

EBay Express! (EE) is a separate, specialty-selling eBay website for buyers who are looking mostly for new, fixed-price goods, only from experienced eBay sellers. The primary purpose of shopping on EE is that all sellers must meet certain qualifications such as meeting eligibility requirements for PayPal's Buyer Protection, having a Feedback Score of 100 at 98 percent positive or higher, and selling in a more conventional e-commerce method (Fixed Price as opposed to Auction-Style). You no longer have to search through all of the listings that include auctions or inexperienced sellers.

Another advantage of EE is that you will be able to shop among many sellers, adding items to your shopping cart along the way. Then once you have finished shopping, you can check out with PayPal and pay for all your items, to all the sellers, at one time. You can find eBay Express! by either going to eBay.com and clicking on the eBay Express! logo or by going directly to www.ebayexpress.com.

Keyword Searches

2.12 "How can I use special characters to narrow my keyword searches?"

A common mistake is to assume that keyword searches on eBay work the same as Internet search engines. It does not matter what order the keywords are in unless they are within "quotes." Searches are not case-sensitive. An upper-, lower-, or mixed-case search produces the same result.

An eBay search does not always correct spelling or suggest alternatives for a misspelled keyword like a Google search does. For certain items and categories, eBay will automatically expand a search and include items that it believes you intended rather than what you actually typed.

This can be either beneficial or annoying. Sometimes you may want to purposely search for listings that have a particular misspelled keyword. Placing the keyword within "quotes" ensures that eBay will not assume your intention and will only display exactly what you have typed.

The following table summarizes how different keyword formatting produces alternate search results for a Nikon camera.

If Desired Search Result Is ...	And the Keywords Are ...	The Search Will Return ...
Listings that contain a particular word	camera	Listings that contain the word camera.
Listings that contain two words	Nikon camera	Listings that contain both words Nikon <u>and</u> camera. Order of the words is not relevant.
Listings that contain words in a particular order	"Nikon camera"	Listings that contain Nikon camera, in that order.
Listings that do not contain certain words	Nikon camera −bag	Listings that contain the words Nikon camera, except those also containing the word bag.
Listings that don't contain several words	Nikon camera −bag −lens −"smart card"	Listings that include Nikon camera but none that *also* include bag, lens, or smart card.
Either a Nikon or Kodak camera, bag, or lens	bag lens (Nikon, Kodak)	Listings that contain either the words Nikon or Kodak <u>and</u> bag <u>and</u> lens.
Listings that contain at least a portion of a word (known as a wildcard)	Photography light*	Using the asterisk * will display listings that contain the words Photography and light, lights, lighting, etc.
Listings that contain a specific spelling	"Nicon" camera	Shows all listings with the misspelled Nicon camera. Buyers sometimes use this method looking for items with little competition because the seller misspelled Nikon as Nicon.

2.13 "Should I use misspelled words in my searches?"

Yes, definitely. The reason is that many sellers are poor spellers and do not use spell check when creating their titles. If you use commonly misspelled keywords, you may find items that have very few bidders. This means less competition and a better chance of winning the item.

2.14 "Can you save your favorite searches?"

Yes, you can save your favorite or more complex searches. After you perform the search, click the **Save this search** button at the top of the results. You can later find, perform, and edit your favorite searches in your **My eBay** tab and then select **Favorite Searches.**

You can also have eBay e-mail you when an item from one of your favorite searches becomes available. Rather than having to search constantly on eBay every few days, you can set up a favorite keyword search to monitor eBay for matching items. If an item appears on eBay with those keywords, you will be automatically notified by e-mail. You only receive one e-mail alert per item, per day even if other items that qualify are added later that day. This notification feature expires six months after you create one.

Bidding

2.15 "If there are two bidders who submit the same highest bid, who wins?"

The winner is the one who placed her bid first. I snipe, which means I place my bids in the last few seconds. Therefore, it is unlikely that my bid will be the first one placed. That is another reason why I bid an odd amount. Two bidders may bid $20, or even $21.50, but it would be rare that the two highest bidders would both bid $21.57.

SEE ALSO   3.2 "Do you recommend bidding an even or odd dollar amount?"

SEE ALSO   3.4 "I lost an auction at the last second. What happened?"

2.16   "Can I retract a bid if I made a mistake or changed my mind and I no longer want the item?"

Yes. However, you should only retract a bid for legitimate reasons such as ...

- You made a mistake when you placed the bid. Note you must make this change by offering a new bid immediately. Select **Site Map** and then select **Bid Retraction** under **Buyer Resources.**

- The seller has changed something in the auction (it should be a significant change) since you bid.

- You have tried to contact the seller with questions and he has not responded.

These activities are tracked by eBay. If you make bid retraction a habit, eBay will contact you. In addition, the number of retractions you make will appear next to your Feedback Score. Therefore, you really do not want to retract a bid unless you absolutely must. Be careful when bidding on eBay and only place bids on an item you truly want at the price you are willing to pay.

2.17   "I just won an item on eBay but now I have buyer's remorse. Can I get out of it?"

Yes, as long as the seller agrees to let you out of it. Your winning bid was a legal contract to buy the item from the seller. The seller may insist that you pay for your item. On the other hand, you may both mutually agree to cancel the transaction.

Be very nice to the seller. You have just made some extra work for her. Now she has to relist the item and file the proper online forms to get her final seller fees back from eBay. If she is not a PowerSeller, she won't get any special feature fees she paid back either.

Contact the seller and explain your remorse. Tell her that you would be happy to agree to a "mutual withdrawal from transaction" so she can get her fees reimbursed. If the seller agrees, she then has to fill out the required online forms and you will be notified about the request for cancellation by an e-mail from eBay and a pop-up alert.

Once you respond that you agree to cancel the transaction, eBay will cancel the sale and the seller will receive a refund for her fees.

Please use this sparingly! Again, eBay is watching. Cancelling transactions is not in the spirit of eBay. If you make this a practice, eBay may suspend your account. Don't forget that the seller has no obligation to allow you to cancel and does not deserve negative feedback if they choose not to allow you out of the sale.

2.18 "Sometimes when I bid on an item, eBay immediately says I have been outbid. This seems suspicious to me. What is going on?"

This is how eBay bidding works. When you place a bid on eBay you are actually using a proxy bidding method, meaning eBay places bids on your behalf. There is no option to this. All bids placed on eBay are by proxy.

The good news is that, with this method, eBay favors you over the seller by only bidding the minimum amount required to be either the high bidder or to reach the reserve price. For example, if an item has no bids and the starting bid is $1, you can enter the highest bid you are willing to pay (say $20) and eBay will place your bid for only $1. The reason is that $1 is the starting bid and therefore the minimum amount required at this time for you to be the high bidder. Only you and eBay know about the remaining $19. If no one else bids on the item, you will win it for $1 even though you entered $20.

If someone else bids later, eBay will automatically place another bid for you that will again be the minimum amount required at that time to keep you as the high bidder. This bidding method will continue until your bid reaches $20, which was your highest bid.

The best strategy using eBay's proxy bidding then is to place, just once, the highest bid you are willing to pay. Then let eBay automatically bid on your behalf throughout the auction. You win it or you lose it. Because eBay will always bid the minimum amount required, you may even end up paying much less than your maximum bid.

2.19 "If someone places a higher bid than mine when I am not logged in to eBay, how will I know that I have been outbid?"

EBay will send an e-mail informing you that you have been outbid. If you have installed the eBay Toolbar, you'll also get a small pop-up on the bottom of your screen telling you that you have been outbid.

SEE ALSO **5.27** *"What is the eBay Toolbar?"*

2.20 "I am interested in an item that is only $1, but the shipping charge is $35. The shipping should be about $5. What should I do?"

The seller is unscrupulous. He is inflating his shipping rate in order to avoid paying his Final Value eBay fees, as the fees are not based on the shipping rate. This upsets me because I play by the rules and pay my fees. These deceitful sellers have an advantage until eBay catches them, and I like to help that process along.

If a seller cheats eBay, he will have no problem cheating you as well. Therefore, do not bid on his item. Instead, report him to eBay's Trust and Safety Department. When viewing the listing, select **Report Item.** From the drop-down menu, select **Listing Policy Violations.** Then under **Detailed Reason,** select **Excessive Shipping and Handling.** Now let eBay deal with the problem.

It is always fun to watch the item disappear from eBay. You know that the seller just got his hand slapped. If he continues this process, he will have his account suspended.

2.21 "How can I be sure the seller is trustworthy before I place a bid?"

There is no foolproof method that can guarantee the seller is reputable. However, there are several areas of the listing that, collectively, will provide you with important clues.

Specifically, I would carefully check the seller's return and payment policies, shipping rates, seller location, her Feedback Score, positive feedback percentage, Detailed Seller Ratings (DSRs), and feedback comments.

Kevin's Seller Approval Test

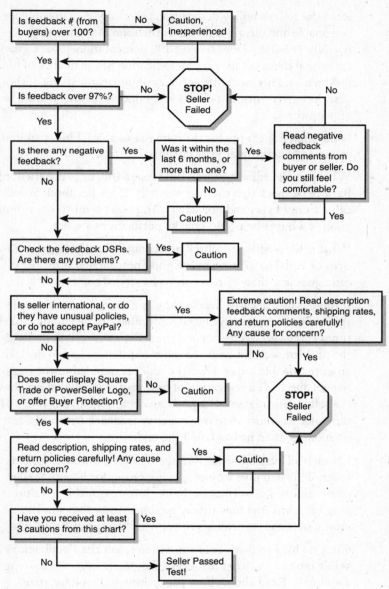

Kevin's Seller Approval Test

The following is Kevin's Seller Approval Test:

- Read the seller's policy descriptions carefully. Are his policies reasonable and clearly written? Is the tone of each policy friendly or harsh? Does he give 100 percent money-back guarantee? All these details give an indication of the quality of his products and his customer service commitment. If any of the descriptions, terms, or policies seem unreasonable, I would be very cautious.

- Is the shipping charge for the item reasonable? This is an indication of honesty or at least fairness.

- What is his Feedback Score? If it is over 100, he is experienced. Be sure to check that the vast majority of his Feedback Scores came from buyers and not sellers. You don't want to know how good of a buyer he is, but how he performs as a seller.

- What is his positive feedback percentage? Anything greater than or equal to 97 percent is a good percentage. If his percentage is less than 97 percent, he has failed the test.

- If there is any negative feedback, was it more than six months ago? Anyone can receive negative feedback occasionally. Sometimes things go wrong beyond the seller's control. Sometimes the problem was not with the seller but that he had to deal with an unreasonable buyer. How the seller responded to the negative feedback is an indication of how professional he is and how the seller will treat you if a problem occurs with your order. If the seller has more than one negative feedback within the last six months, then he has failed the test.

- Check his Detailed Seller Ratings (DSRs) if available for this seller. This will give a more specific rating for how the seller communicates, describes his items, how reasonable his shipping rates are, and how timely he ships. You can hover the mouse over the star ratings to see what the specific rating is.

- Click on his Feedback Score and then select the **Feedback as a seller** tab to view what his recent customers have been saying about him. Read about three pages deep and look for statements like "fast shipping" and "item just as described." These comments indicate honesty and attention to detail. If you see comments such as "item was as described but it took two weeks to receive it," or "seller ignored my e-mails," read a few pages deeper. If more comments similar to this appear, the seller may not be competent and you should proceed only with extreme caution. If the seller has received negative feedback recently, be sure to find and read those comments.

- Does he display the PowerSeller logo? If yes, this reveals a serious seller.

PowerSeller Logo

- Does the seller display the Square Trade logo in his listings? If yes, the seller has been approved by Square Trade as a preferred and trusted seller. Note that many honest sellers do not participate in Square Trade. I would never rule out a seller if he is not associated with Square Trade. However, if you find one that is, this is a terrific endorsement.

Square Trade Logo

- Is the seller located outside of the United States (check next to the price to see the Item Location)? If he is not located in the United States, be *very* careful. Many scams on eBay are from international sellers. In the past, some have listed inexpensive items but did not indicate any shipping amount. Then after you purchased their item, you were shocked to see the invoice that has a $500 shipping charge!

Some sellers try to get around this by listing the item location as United States when they are actually registered in another country. Double-check the seller's location in the **Meet the Seller** box (it also shows whether they're registered as an individual or a business). If the registered country is different than the item's location, the seller has failed the test.

- Does the seller's information box claim that the item qualifies for PayPal Buyer Protection? If yes, you know you have protection if you pay for the item with PayPal (as you always should for maximum protection). If the seller does not offer this protection, you are at risk if something goes wrong. For me, this is a dealbreaker unless that type of item cannot qualify for Buyer Protection. If you decide to proceed, use extreme caution.

- Has the seller stated that he does not accept PayPal? If yes, use extreme caution. Many sellers gripe about PayPal fees and choose to offer another valid choice of payment. So while the seller may be legitimate, understand that, once again, if you pay outside of PayPal you have lost your protection. Personally, that seller fails for me because I want Buyer Protection.

If everything looks favorable at this point, you have done as much background checking as is practical. I would feel comfortable with a seller who passed this test. If instead it has provided you with three or more cautions, the seller has failed the test. While this test may sometimes mistakenly fail a reputable seller, it will identify most of the disreputable ones. If a seller fails the test, look for competing sellers who offer the same product at a similar price. If a seller has failed the test but you choose to bid on a particular item because it is rare, understand that your risk of experiencing some sort of problem is considerable.

Payments

2.22 "How long do I have to pay for an auction?"

The seller has to wait seven days before he can file an Unpaid Item Dispute (UPI). Each seller may have different leniencies. If there is any reason you cannot pay within that time frame, contact the seller immediately and explain the situation. Never bid on an item that you do not intend to pay for.

2.23 "Should I pay for insurance or tracking?"

I sometimes choose to pay for insurance depending on the value of the item. I would also consider insurance if the item is breakable.

I would not pay for any tracking or Delivery Confirmation. The reason is that the USPS does not provide tracking for Priority Mail or Parcel Post during transit. They will only inform you or the seller when the item has been delivered. That is why it is called Delivery Confirmation and not tracking. As the buyer, you will know when it has been delivered, therefore there is no need to pay for the service. Plus, to qualify for PayPal Seller Protection, the seller must use a trackable shipping method that shows Delivery Confirmation. The seller should therefore be paying for this (if they print their postage online, Delivery Confirmation is required anyway).

Other carriers such as DHL, UPS, and FedEx provide true tracking so you know where your package is throughout transit to you. Their tracking is included in the shipping price so you should not have to pay extra for this service.

2.24 "I don't have a PayPal account. Should I pay with a check, cashier's check, or money order?"

No. If you pay with any method outside of PayPal, you have lost your Buyer Protection. If the seller accepts PayPal payments, you can pay for your item with a major credit card.

2.25 "But what if the seller doesn't accept PayPal payments?"

Find another seller. He may indeed be a reputable seller and offer a legitimate alternative payment method; it is also true that if you pay for the item with a credit card you will have some protection from your credit card company. However, personally I will not pay for an item outside of PayPal because I lose all my Buyer Protection benefits. See question 2.21.

2.26 "Can I pay for my items with an eCheck?"

Yes, you can pay for an eBay item with an eCheck using PayPal as long as the seller accepts it. An eCheck is an electronic transfer of funds from a checking account to the seller's PayPal account. It works the same way a paper check does and usually needs four business days to clear, but can take up to two weeks.

SEE ALSO 1.35 "What is an eCheck?"

2.27 "I don't feel comfortable paying for my items online. Can't I just pay with a check or money order?"

You are going to have to get over this. Payments online are safer than almost any other form of payment.

Many people who feel uncomfortable buying items online think nothing of handing a waiter their credit card in a restaurant. The waiter can easily make a note of your card and security numbers or swipe the card into a personal reader. When you write a check, you are giving your account and routing numbers along with your signature to any number of people in a processing center.

Paying for an eBay item with an online transaction through PayPal is one of the most secure payments you can make. All private financial data is encrypted with the latest security protocols. Your payment is also protected if your seller offers PayPal's Buyer Protection. If you write a check or money order, you have lost that protection. In fact, eBay no longer allows payments using written checks.

SEE ALSO 1.33 "What is PayPal's Buyer Protection Program?"

SEE ALSO 2.24 "I don't have a PayPal account. Should I pay with a check, cashier's check, or money order?"

3 Power Buying

As buyers gain experience, they begin to study auctions they have won or lost to determine how they can improve their chance of winning. They discover patterns and then begin to develop their own strategies. Often at this point, more advanced questions arise. This section provides the answers to the questions most often asked by power buyers.

Bidding

3.1 "When is the best time to buy items on eBay?"

The quick answer is to buy when you have the least competition. But here are some guidelines:

Best Time of Year. If the item you desire is seasonal, the best time to buy is during the off-season. Buy snowboards in July and swimsuits in January. Generally, the summer is a great time to buy. Most of your buying competition is on vacation or outside doing other things. In particular, July is a great time to buy. Conversely, it is usually a lousy time to sell unless you sell summer related items.

Best Day and Time. I can't recommend a particular day although I seem to notice that Friday nights are particularly good for buying men's items. I can only conclude that men are doing other things on a Friday night rather than browsing eBay. This means you will have less competition. Look for items that end in the middle of the night. Because most bids are placed at the last minute, items that end in the middle of the night (Pacific time) will have very few last-minute bidders. Does this mean you have to set your alarm clock to get up at 3:00 A.M. to place your bid? No. Use sniping services (mentioned later) to bid on your behalf.

Best Time in the Auction. The last two seconds of the auction. But make sure you're on the bid confirmation page, not just entering the bid, or the auction will end before your bid and confirmation registers.

3.2 "Do you recommend bidding an even or odd dollar amount?"

New eBay buyers tend to bid "even," and experienced buyers bid "odd." I bid odd plus just a bit more.

For example, if I am willing to bid a maximum of $20 for a certain item, I know that inexperienced bidders will be bidding $20, $21, or $21.50. The bid I would place would be $21.57. You would not believe how many items I have won by a few cents!

3.3 "When do you place your bid?"

With two seconds to go in the auction. That way, no bidders who are manually bidding against me have enough time to react. It is called "sniping."

If you do not or cannot snipe, then bid the highest amount you are willing to pay and let eBay's proxy bidding service bid for you. In many cases, you may win the item for much less than the full amount you bid.

3.4 "I lost an auction at the last second. What happened?"

This is especially aggravating to new buyers. You were a victim of a snipe by an experienced buyer. Sniping is not only allowed on eBay, but I encourage you to do it as well.

If you are at a live auction, when is the best time to place your bid? It is when the auctioneer is just about to drop the gavel. Otherwise, your early bids raise the price of the item and, in a sense, you are raising the bid price on yourself. You should use the same bidding method for eBay auctions.

By only placing my bid with two seconds to go ...

- I have not raised the price of the item during the length of the auction nor the perceived interest in the item by increasing the number of bids.

- My competition does not even know I am there (I'm the tiger hiding in the grass).

- No one who is trying to place a bid manually can counter my bid within two seconds.

How do I place a bid in the last two seconds? With a very fast Internet service or by using sniping service providers. If using a sniping service, your bid is sent from the sniping provider's server to eBay's servers over high-speed Internet lines. Two seconds is plenty of time to arrive in the server-to-server technical world. It is impossible to respond to another bid manually within two seconds.

Of course, you can still lose to a bidder who places a higher bid, but you can guarantee that no one can manually respond to your bid in the last two seconds. This greatly increases your chance of beating inexperienced buyers and winning the item.

When sniping yourself (with a fast connection) or when using a sniping service, remember to bid the maximum amount you are willing to pay for the item. You win or lose based on your bid amount, not on someone being able to counter your bid.

Some of the more popular sniping providers include the following: www.auctionstealer.com, www.esnipe.com, www.auctionsnipe.com, www.bidnip.com, www.powersnipe.com, and www.bidslammer.com. Most offer a few free snipes a month and then a small monthly fee if you want to place more snipes. I don't necessarily recommend one over the other. Check them all out—compare their services and rates to see which one meets your requirements.

3.5 "How can I avoid getting caught up in the frenzy of the auction and bidding too much?"

First, you need to determine the value of the item on eBay. I do this by using HammerTap (www.hammertap.com/studentrate) to see what these items have been selling for in the past 90 days. I determine never to bid above that value. I also check HammerTap to see the best time and day to end an auction and I avoid those times. I can also see what days bring the fewest bids and look for an auction that ends during that day.

Next, using a sniping service, I place my maximum bid just once for the amount I am willing to spend, with two seconds to go in the auction. I am not even watching the auction when it is about to end so I am not tempted to jump in the frenzy. Determine your maximum bid and bid that amount just once. You win or you lose. If you lose, you can try it again next week.

POWERSELLER TIP

Here is another bit of advice for controlling emotional bidding. I learned this lesson from working in the Chicago loop for five years. Never chase a bus. The reason is that another bus is just about to come around the corner. The same is true with eBay buying. Unless the item is very rare or I need it right away, I never chase an auction. There will be another auction for that item next week, or the week after.

Potential Product or Seller Problems

3.6 "What is shill bidding?"

Shill bidding occurs when a seller has a friend bid on her item in order to run up the price. This is not only against eBay policy, it is actually illegal. Never try to bid on your own item or agree to bid up an item for a friend. If you are caught, your account will be immediately suspended and eBay may choose to report you to your state's attorney general.

3.7 "I suspect I was a victim of shill bidding. What should I do?"

Actually, this practice is not as common as you might think. EBay has developed very sophisticated proprietary software that searches for this type of activity. They actually track the ISP and computer addresses of buyers and sellers and check for certain unusual and repeating activities. A disreputable seller might get away with it for a while, but either eBay will eventually catch him or an unhappy bidder will turn him in.

Remember that just because several bids came in at the last minute does not mean the seller was shilling. This is how most auctions end. If you truly think you have been a victim of shill bidding, you can report the incident to eBay's Trust and Safety Department.

3.8 "Are you saying I can't bid on a friend or family member's item?"

Correct. Just say no. EBay allows you to purchase a friend's listing by using the Buy It Now feature only. For me, however, I will not even do that. I do not want to even risk the possible appearance of shilling.

3.9 "How can I know for sure that a collectible item is authentic?"

You can't. However, there are a few things you should do before you bid. Check the seller's reputation carefully by using my Seller Approval Test in question 2.21. Read several pages of comments from their buyers.

Check with the seller to see if he has a certificate of authenticity from one of eBay's approved authenticators. You can learn more about this service by selecting the **Help** link and typing **authentication and grading.**

Search eBay and the Internet and try to determine the value for the item. If the item is being sold at a ridiculously low price, that is a red flag. It may be a great deal, but it is more likely a fake.

If the item is commonly copied with fakes or knock-offs such as a Gucci bag, conduct an Internet search and type "Gucci bag" along with the keywords "fake," "fraud," or "counterfeit." This will produce information about that subject as well as find legitimate sellers of the item online. Study their sites for information on how to detect a fake.

Note that reproductions of most items are not allowed to be sold on eBay. Exceptions may include items such as reproductions of coins. Even then, the seller must clearly describe the coin as a reproduction.

Sometimes the seller may even unknowingly sell a fake. If you are bidding on an item that is easy to replicate, just know that you are at risk. If the seller gives you any cause for concern, find another seller.

3.10 "The item arrived broken, or the seller sent the wrong item, or the item doesn't work, or the seller never shipped the item. What do I do?"

Give the seller the benefit of the doubt. Sometimes things go wrong and the seller is not at fault.

E-mail the seller using the **Ask seller a question** link (in the "Meet the Seller" section of the listing) and explain the problem. Her response will tell you whether you should be concerned or not. Give her two or three days to respond. If you don't hear back from her within that time, e-mail the seller again with the same message and give her another two days.

If you still have not heard from her, consider calling her. Open the **Advanced Search** page, select **Find a Member** and then **Contact Information**. If you have had a recent transaction with the seller, eBay will provide you with her phone number. Note that if you request her phone number, she will receive an e-mail from eBay providing her with your phone number as well. She will certainly be surprised when you call her!

At all times be very courteous and professional. Do not make threats or become belligerent. If you cannot get in touch with her or convince her to fix the problem, see the next question.

3.11 "The seller refuses to solve the problem with our transaction. What do I do?"

If you didn't receive the product, file an "Item not Received" dispute with eBay. Go to your My eBay, and under My eBay Views, select **Dispute Console**.

Check to see if the item qualified for PayPal Buyer Protection. If the item qualified, file a Buyer Protection claim with PayPal. Login to your PayPal account and select the **Security** link at the top of the page. Then follow the instructions for filing a dispute with the Purchase Protection Program.

Power Buying Methods and Tools

3.12 "What is the best tip you can give that would help me become a better power buyer?"

You should conduct research on eBay to determine the value of the item before you place any bid. Rather than guessing the value, find out what the item has been selling for on eBay recently and how common or rare the item is.

1. Select the **Advanced Search** link on the Primary Search tool bar.

2. Enter the keywords for the item you desire and place a check in the box labeled **Show Completed listings only.**

3. Click the **Search** button. EBay will now display all listings containing those keywords that have completed (ended) in the last two weeks.

Study the prices closely in the search results. A listing displayed with a green-colored price means that the item sold at that price. A listing that displays a red-colored price means that the price was what the seller was asking, but the item did not sell.

After studying this list carefully, you can determine what the true value for the item has been over the last two weeks. This information will prevent you from overbidding on the item. You can also determine if the item is a common item with multiple future buying opportunities if you decide to pass on this one now.

If it is a popular item with many listings, check to see when the lowest prices occurred. This will help determine which current auctions end on the same day of the week and approximate time, and when you are most likely to find the best deal.

SEE ALSO **4.34 "How should I conduct eBay research?"**

3.13 "What is a Second Chance Offer?"

Second Chance Offers (SCO) are not only legitimate, but they are a great way for buyers to get a fantastic deal on an item that they bid on but did not win. EBay allows sellers to make SCOs to their nonwinning bidders if they have additional quantities of the item or if the winner did not pay for the item.

The SCO enables the bidder to purchase the item for the highest bid he made during the auction. This strategy is beneficial to the non-winning bidders who may be able to pay several dollars less than the winning bid. It is also beneficial to the seller who can quickly move quantities of the same product without paying for additional listing fees (they only pay the Final Value Fee).

If you have received a Second Chance Offer, you should first ensure that it is legitimate and not a spoof e-mail. Login to your eBay account, go to your My eBay page, and check your **My Messages** link. Any legitimate SCOs for you will appear there. If it is, you were probably just offered a great deal! But know that they do expire after a seller-specified time, or when the quantity runs out. For example, the seller sends nine SCOs but only has six of the item. The first six respondents get the items and the other three SCOs expire immediately.

SEE ALSO   **5.18** "How many days should I give my bidders to respond when I provide a Second Chance Offer?"

3.14   "Are there tools that can help me conduct more in-depth research?"

Yes. These tools are used by sellers in order to determine the value of an item and study how best to create their listings. However, a buyer can also use the tools to quickly determine the value of an item before he bids. There are two research tools that are most popular among eBay members: HammerTap and eBay Marketplace Research by Terapeak.

Each tool has particular features and benefits compared to the others. Many serious sellers use HammerTap because of its sophisticated design and the level of detail from its reports.

SEE ALSO   **5.26** "Which product-analysis tools do you use and recommend?"

4 Selling Basics

There are many different types of eBay sellers. Most begin their selling in order to get rid of a few things they have accumulated but no longer want. Inherited items may need to be liquidated. Some sellers are hobbyists, while others want supplemental income. Business owners may decide to expand their sales channels. There are also sellers who make eBay their full-time business.

Each type of seller has different goals, needs, and motivation. However, they all share similar eBay selling experiences. As sellers progress through their eBay journey, they will occasionally run into a few problems, speed bumps, detours, or outright roadblocks. This chapter addresses the types of questions and problems nearly all eBay sellers will eventually encounter.

Before You Sell

Before you begin selling on eBay, there are a few tools that are a "must have" for every eBay seller. Primarily you will need a digital camera to take pictures of the items for sale to display in your listings. You should also purchase a postal scale to accurately determine the weight, so you can calculate the shipping rate when you create your listings. Finally, take advantage of free eBay/USPS co-branded Priority Mail shipping boxes available to order from the USPS.

SEE ALSO   8.1   "What camera do you recommend for eBay photography?"

SEE ALSO   9.9   "How do I get those free co-branded eBay/USPS Priority Mail boxes?"

SEE ALSO   9.24   "What type of postal scale do you recommend and where can I get one?"

Your First Few Sales

If you are new to eBay selling, you no doubt have many questions. Before we get to questions that are more specific, I have provided a few recommendations to help guide you through your first few sales:

- At first, it is more important to learn how to sell and do order fulfillment and shipping than it is to make money. You need to learn the steps of the process including research, listing creation, payment, shipping, and feedback.

- For your first few listings, start with something simple like a popular used book in good condition (such as a newly released book you've already finished reading). Everyone understands what a book is. Your mistakes will be minimal.

- If you are completely new to eBay selling, I suggest you read a beginning eBay selling book or attend an eBay-approved class. You can find a class near you at www.poweru.net/ebay/student/searchindex.asp.

- Double-check your listings immediately after they post on eBay and before a bid is received. Correct any mistakes immediately with the **Revise your item** link.

- After about a dozen listings and positive feedback, you are now more experienced and confident to move on to more profitable items.

- Progress slowly and with caution. Don't jump from selling a book to selling a car! Start with items under $20, then move to items under $50, then $100, and so on.

- Read this entire chapter (especially see questions 4.37 and 4.68) and also review the components for a successful eBay business in question 7.12.

Writing Descriptions

4.1 "What is your advice for writing a good description?"

Think like a buyer when you write your description. You want to minimize any confusion by answering the questions buyers will often have about the item. Ask yourself, "If I were interested in this item, what

would I need to know before I placed a bid?" Then proceed to write
the description based on your questions. Be sure to cover these basics:

- What is the item for sale?
- What is included in the listing (any accessories)?
- What is the condition of the item?
- What is the color and what are the dimensions?
- List briefly any defects or flaws.
- Are there any particular characteristics or an interesting history that should be mentioned?
- State the benefits and features.
- If the item is technical, electrical, or mechanical, list all technical specifications in a bullet list.
- Include your shipping rates, payment, and return policies.

Create an eye-catching descriptive heading using a larger type and a
different font than the text. Select a color, perhaps blue for the heading, and then write the text in B&W.

Buyers have short attention spans. Keep your descriptions brief yet
complete. Don't write one long paragraph. It is too hard to read. A few
short paragraphs, or even bullets, are better. Place the most important
or interesting information first. Keep the message positive and informative. Write in a conversational style and do not WRITE IN ALL
CAPS. Always check your spelling and grammar.

Study the descriptions of the top sellers of the particular item you are
selling when you conduct your research. However, don't simply
rewrite their descriptions. Make your text unique so it will stand alone
from the others. Learn how professional advertising copy writers
create descriptions by scanning product catalogs and online websites
that carry similar items.

4.2 "What should I write if my item has a flaw in it?"

You should be honest and describe the flaw. If it is a collectible item,
take a picture of the flaw and in the description write, "The plate is
in perfect condition except that it has a very small chip on the bottom

that measures half an inch. Please refer to picture #3, which shows a close-up of the chip."

Do you think this will hurt your sales? No, in fact it produces quite the opposite effect. It shows that you are an honest seller. Even if the buyer decides to pass on that plate, she will most likely look at your other items or return to purchase another item from you because she believes she can trust you.

Never try to hide a flaw. You risk bad feedback. At the same time, don't dwell on the flaw, either. Simply mention it and move on to a more positive message.

4.3 "Can I write my descriptions ahead of time in MS Word and then do a copy/paste to either the Sell Your Item form or Turbo Lister?"

I don't recommend it. The reason is that when you copy text from Microsoft Word and paste it, the text tends to bring some Microsoft code (called tags) along with it that does not interact well with eBay code. Many times when I have tried this, and then tried to edit the text, I had real difficulties with text size, bold, and fonts. They seem to change randomly and, no matter what I do, I cannot change them back. I end up having to type it all over again anyway in Turbo Lister or the Sell Your Item (SYI) form.

I have had better luck with copy/paste using MS Notepad, as that application removes the tags. Therefore, you can write your description in MS Word, copy/paste it to Notepad, and then copy/paste it again into a Turbo Lister or SYI listing.

Understand that Notepad will also remove any enhancements to the text such as bold or bullets, plus these are two extra steps in the process. Therefore, you will most likely have the fewest problems if you simply write your description at the time of listing creation in either the SYIF or in Turbo Lister.

4.4 "What should I state in my return policies?"

Think of the Golden Rule and write the type of policies that you would like to see if you were the buyer. A "100% Money-Back Guarantee" encourages me to buy, but when I see "No refunds or returns," I tend to look for another seller.

EBay has mandatory rules requiring sellers to state their return and handling time policies. The rules do not require you to accept returns, but you must state what your policies are. You should have a different return policy for a rare, one of a kind item than for an item where you have several in stock. Look at the policies of the top sellers of your item. Take a bit from each one and create your own hybrid policy.

Be sure to write that the buyer must contact you first before she returns the item. State clearly who will pay for the shipping if it needs to be returned. If an item you shipped arrived broken or defective, you should pay for the return shipping. If the buyer wanted to return the item because she didn't like the color, she will pay for return shipping. State that the item must be returned in a condition suitable for resale.

Finally, don't write lengthy policies. Even if they are not negative policies, as a buyer I don't want to see a long list of rules. My feeling is that if the seller is that uptight, then I don't want to deal with him. I am looking for a seller with great return policies and a customer service commitment just in case something goes wrong. Again, imagine you are the buyer and think as she would when you write your policies.

4.5 "Can I copy another seller's description?"

No, don't be tempted to do that. You can read what others are writing in their descriptions before you write yours, but never copy anyone's description. Always write your own.

Listing Creation

4.6 "How do I know what to set the price for on a Fixed Price listing?"

Do your research and see what the average selling price (ASP) for the item has been recently on eBay. Then add about 10–15 percent to the ASP for items sold at auction. Note that this is not an exact formula. It depends on many factors including how popular the item is. If you have several of the same items in stock, you may need to experiment with a few trial listings in order to determine where that emotional leap from bidding to wanting to buy it right now will occur.

4.7 "How can I increase the exposure and improve the number of hits for my listing?"

Assuming you have terrific keywords already (see question 4.18), then you can increase visibility by using the Listing Upgrade options available when creating your listing. These would include the following:

- **Gallery Picture** (free): The thumbnail picture that is next to your listing title when a buyer performs a keyword search. Ensure that you have a professional-looking gallery picture.

- **10-Day Listing** (40¢): Extends the listing to 10 days instead of the standard 7-day listings.

- **Bold** ($1): Changes the type from standard to Bold and makes the type stand out from other listings.

- **Border** ($3): Places a colored box around your listing.

- **Highlight** ($5): Makes the listing stand out by using a background color similar to using a highlighter on text in a book.

- **Gallery Featured** ($19.95): Places your item above the general picture gallery in a special, featured gallery area.

- **Featured Plus!** ($9.95 to $24.95): Places your item at the top of the category list on the search results page.

- **List Internationally:** Consider making your listing available to international buyers.

- **Maintain a Great DSR Feedback Score:** Your Detailed Seller Ratings (DSR) will determine how high your item is placed in eBay's Best Match search results.

4.8 "Do you use Listing Upgrades in your listings?"

These options can be costly, so I use them sparingly. However, I do use them when I am selling expensive items or sometimes when there is a lot of competition. I do use 10-day auctions frequently for more expensive items. I feel that the extra three days (and two weekends) of exposure is worth the additional fee.

I don't usually add many frilly enhancements. I always make sure I have a great gallery picture so a buyer who is just scrolling through the category or using the "snapshot" view of search results may be attracted to my listing. I also may use a template so all my related listings have the same look.

I have tried Bold, Border, and Highlight a few times but usually with no significant difference in the results. I can't recommend them because of their cost ($1, $3, $5 accordingly).

If you use several pictures in your listings, you should choose the Picture Pack enhancement. It gives a discount rate for 6 to 12 photos that can be supersized.

I sometimes use Featured Plus, which places an item at the top of the category for the length of the listing. When I do this, I always make sure it is for a 10-day listing. I usually receive five to seven times more hits than normal. I usually use it as advertising to draw customers to my listing and then send them to my store to purchase other items. This strategy has usually worked well for me, but I don't recommend it for beginners. You need to understand your products and competition thoroughly before spending $9.95–$24.95 on a single listing. I would not recommend this feature if you do not have a fully stocked eBay Store, unless your item is very expensive and you can justify the cost.

Remember that the purpose of enhancements is to set your listing apart from all your competition. You can also accomplish this by using different gallery pictures and subtitles. These alternatives are significantly cheaper than using Bold, Border Highlight, or other enhancements. With all that in mind, experiment.

The best way to make a decision about whether a Listing Upgrade is worth the money is by using HammerTap. In just a few seconds, HammerTap will research eBay's historical database and display all listings that had similar keywords and ended within the last 90 days. You can then compare standard listings with those that used Listing Upgrades (if any were used). In most cases, you can then see the benefit of the upgrade and determine whether it is worth the cost, rather than having to guess.

SEE ALSO 5.26 "Which product-analysis tools do you use and recommend?"

4.9 "Do you recommend using subtitles?"

Yes, if I think it will give me an edge on my competition. The charge is 50¢, so I don't use subtitles on low-priced items.

As a reminder, subtitles are not searchable using a standard search, which is what most buyers use. However, if I can grab a buyer's attention with an eye-catching subtitle such as "Free Shipping" or "Bonus Item Included" and the item is valuable, then it is worth 50¢.

4.10 "Do you add a handling fee to your shipping rate?"

Yes, I do. I feel it is appropriate to charge a reasonable fee to pack the item and, in some cases, take it to the Post Office. I usually charge about $2 for handling and materials. I don't separate these fees in my listing; I give one S&H price. If the item will cost $5 to ship, state that the "Shipping and Handling rate is $6.95."

The ability to have eBay automatically add a handling cost to your shipping rate is available only when using the Calculated Rate shipping option. Sellers who use Flat Rates should include any handling charges as part of their total rate. Handling rates, even for international shipments, should be kept low and reasonable, usually $2–$3 or less per package.

SEE ALSO 9.22 "How can I determine how much to charge for shipping?"

4.11 "How can I hide my hit counter?"

When you are listing your item, one of the last steps is to add or hide a hit counter. It is important for you to have a hit counter because it gives you a good idea of how popular your item is. For example, if your hit counter is at 3 for a 7-day listing, your item has limited market or your customers aren't clicking through or can't find you, so check your keywords. If your hit counter is at 100 or more for a 7-day listing, you have a popular item that will draw many interested buyers.

You will be amazed at which items are popular and which aren't. This information is invaluable to you as an eBay seller in determining which products to order/sell or drop to keep your business profitable and growing.

Some sellers choose to hide their hit counters. They do this mostly to keep this information from their competition. It is also an indicator to your buyers how much competition they have and may influence them to hold off bidding on your item if the hits are low.

To hide my hit counters, when filling out the Sell Your Item form, I choose the option to keep the counter hidden. You can view your hits under your My eBay page and click on your auction under the **Active** link. Toward the top of the listing, your hits are the number next to **Visits**.

4.12 "What do you think of using colored backgrounds and fancy templates for listings?"

I sometimes use templates in order to give all my listings a similar theme. However, don't get too cute. Sometimes the templates can distract from the message.

I rarely use a colored background to the text. We are all used to reading in black and white, so make your text black with a white background. I have seen some backgrounds that were so dark that I could hardly read the words. I recently saw a black text on a dark-brown background in a magazine. The article was impossible to read. I can't imagine what the editors were thinking when they approved it. Why take that chance on your item's description just to make it pretty or different?

I have seen some background templates that looked very nice and gave the item an enhanced perceived value. If you choose a colored background, just be sure it enhances and does not conflict with the text.

4.13 "How does pre-filled information work?"

When listing popular media items such as books, CDs, and DVDs, eBay allows you to enter a unique identifier and they will provide a stock photo and description. There is no charge for this feature.

While this seems to be a good thing, there are two potential problems. First, this makes your listing look like all the others with no distinguishing differences. Second, sometimes the information, edition, or even picture is wrong.

When I use pre-filled information I always make a few changes to the text—especially the first paragraph. I also double-check that the information eBay has provided is correct.

4.14 "How can I use Item Specifics in a listing?"

If item-specific selections are available for the item you are selling, eBay will provide additional fields or drop-down menus with selections such as condition, size, color, make, model, or technical specifications. If you do not include item specifics in your listings, your item will not show up in a buyer's Product Finder Item Specific search.

For example, a buyer may not know what brand or model camera she wants, only that she needs a new digital camera with certain features. She clicks on the **Cameras and Photo** category on eBay, and then, using eBay's Product Finder search box, selects additional item specifics such as resolution, condition, and optical zoom to narrow her search. EBay then displays all cameras that meet the buyer's specifications. Note that the Item Specifics option is not available for all items, but is available for most of the popular media items.

Also, eBay uses selections you make in Item Specifics to bring up items in the search results that don't actually have the buyer's search word in the title. So if a buyer searches for a strapless dress and you didn't put the word "strapless" in the title but did select it in the Item Specifics, it will still appear in the search results. This is a huge reason to use Item Specifics whenever it is available when creating your listing.

4.15 "How can I insert a photo into my listing?"

When using the Sell Your Item form during listing creation, one of the steps will provide you with a page to insert your photos. You begin by first clicking on the **Add a Photo** button. When the browse window appears, select the proper file folder and filename for the photo you have already saved in your computer.

The first photo in an eBay listing is free. Each additional photo is 15¢. The fees for multiple photos in multiple listings can quickly accumulate. So you need to decide whether additional photos are indeed necessary. Most ordinary items, even expensive items, probably need only one or two photos. Collectible items, however, may need several. In this case, choose the Picture Pack option of 1–6 pictures for 75¢ or 7–12 pictures for $1. This upgrade also comes with a supersize feature for the pictures.

Never copy and paste a photo from another seller's listing. This could lead to possible account suspension. Always take your own photos. Also, never copy a photo from a manufacturer's website unless you are an authorized dealer and have received permission to use the photos.

4.16 "How do I relist an item?"

Not every item sells on eBay the first time. You have also spent a lot of time creating your listing. The good news is that if the item doesn't sell, you don't have to create it all over again.

The item will be held for your review in the **Unsold** link of your My eBay page. To relist the item, select the item, click the **Relist** button, revise it as needed, and then resubmit it to eBay.

You will not be charged an Insertion Fee the first time you relist an item. All other fees, such as Listing Upgrades, will still be charged.

Note that you can also relist items that have sold using the same method. For example, maybe you have five items that are the same. After the first item sells, select the **Sold** link instead of **Unsold,** and choose the **Relist** button.

4.17 "Should I relist an unsold item right away?"

I have found that my relist items tend to have a better sell-through rate if I wait several days before I resubmit them. My opinion is that if I resubmit the item immediately, the buyers who will find it this week are probably the same ones who saw it last week and rejected it. If I wait several days or even a few weeks, I will have new buyers and a better chance that the item will sell.

EBay will hold the item in my Unsold section for 90 days. So I sometimes wait two to four weeks or longer before I resubmit the item. My only exception is the summer months. Summer is usually a slow time to sell, so if my item did not sell in May, I may only wait one or two weeks and try it again so I am not trying to sell it in July.

Titles and Keywords

4.18 "What are your suggestions for writing a great title?"

The keywords you use to make up your title are the most important components for a successful listing. You need the best possible keywords in your title that buyers may use to search for your item. So my advice is don't guess. Do your research on eBay to find the best-performing listings for that item and determine what keywords those sellers used.

As you are narrowing your keywords, know that the listing title has a limitation of 55 characters. All characters count, including spaces and punctuation, so do not waste valuable character space by using commas, periods, or exclamation marks. Use all 55 characters if possible.

The keywords are not case sensitive. It also does not matter what order the keywords are in or whether they are grammatically correct. However, it will be easier for your buyer to quickly understand your title if the keywords are arranged in a manner that makes sense.

Your title will be easier to read if you do not type in ALL CAPS, but rather Mixed Case. Then if you need a particular keyword to stand out, type that word in all capitals, such as NEW.

POWERSELLER TIP

A common mistake new eBay sellers make is to write a title as if it were an advertising headline. A great title simply consists of the best keywords possible that buyers will use to find your item.

4.19 "How can I find the most commonly used keywords for the item I am selling?"

I use the sites listed here. I simply enter the primary keywords for the item I am selling. These sites will then show me what other related keywords are also most commonly used by buyers when conducting an Internet search for that item. Here are some keyword finding tools:

- http://pulse.ebay.com
- http://keyword.ebay.com
- https://adwords.google.com/select/KeywordToolExternal
- Yahoo!'s keyword finder: http://tinyurl.com/58y7c5
- www.wordtracker.com

4.20 "I have heard that I should use misspelled words in my title. Wouldn't that make me look dumb?"

I don't care if I look dumb if I can beat my competition using carefully selected, misspelled keywords as a strategy to get more hits. Would you agree there are many eBay buyers that are poor spellers? Do you think these buyers could possibly misspell the brand name of popular items? If you only use keywords that are spelled correctly for items that are commonly misspelled, your listings will not appear on a search to all those buyers who can't spell.

If you won the spelling bee then this may be difficult for you. My advice is to get over it. The point of this is not to show the world whether or not you can spell but to get the maximum amount of hits for your listing. Therefore, if the item you sell is commonly and routinely misspelled, use the correct spelling of the brand name plus the most common way it is misspelled. Now you can capture both types of spellers.

Remember, I am not saying you should have misspelled keywords in your title just for the sake of it. I am only talking about using the commonly misspelled brand names of items. For example, a Brett Favre football may be commonly misspelled by potential buyers conducting a search as Brett Farve. Your title then would include both keywords Favre and Farve.

For help with this process, go to www.typobid.com or www.fatfinger.com. You can type the correct spelling of a word and these sites will show you the most common misspellings of that word.

Now you must get over this dummy thing. If anything, you are showing people you are smart by capturing both types of buyers. If your
competitors are too proud to misspell their keywords and you beat
them by purposely including commonly misspelled keywords, then
you are not the dummy.

4.21 "Should I use eye-catching keywords in my titles like L@@K and Wow!"

I see this quite a bit with new sellers. They use words such as "L@@K,
WOW," or write advertising titles such as, "We offer the best deals on
eBay!"

Think like a buyer searching for your item. No buyer is going to
type as one of their keywords, L@@K, WOW, we, offer, the, best, or
deals! Sellers who do this are missing the point of the title. It is not an
advertisement. It should be made up of excellent keywords that will
provide the most search hits.

4.22 "What is keyword spamming?"

All keywords used in the title must be relevant to the item being sold.
For example, if a seller is listing a pair of sunglasses, he cannot use
keywords such as iPod, cell phone, or LCD TV in order to receive
more buyer search hits. This is known as keyword spamming and the
item will be found and cancelled by eBay's automated anti-spamming
software.

4.23 "Should I use abbreviations in my titles such as BIN, NWT, NIB?"

EBay seems to have its own "eBay-speak" language of multiple abbreviations that many sellers and buyers use and understand. In the
previous examples, Buy It Now (BIN), New With Tags (NWT), and
New In Box (NIB) are frequently used.

Are they useful? If these acronyms are commonly used in the particular category that you are selling in, then they may be useful and they
may even be used as part of the buyer's keyword search. For example,
buyers may prefer clothes that are NWT.

However, if you are selling items in categories that do not normally use these acronyms, the chances are that the buyers will not search for them or even understand what they mean. Do your research and see if the top sellers are using them.

Never trade a good keyword for an acronym. I would only use acronyms if I had exhausted all good keywords and still had a few characters left. By far, the best keyword to use instead of an acronym is the word NEW (assuming your item is new). Just about every listing will produce better results with the word NEW as the first word of the keywords. There is a big difference in the value of a "new" smoking pipe compared with a "used" one (yuck). Buyers of those collectibles will definitely use the word NEW in their searches.

Remember that except for the word NEW, use abbreviations only if you have used all your good keywords and have extra characters. You can find a complete listing of all of eBay's official abbreviations and acronyms by selecting the **Help** link and typing **acronym** in the search box.

Selling Formats

4.24 "What are the different types of listing formats?"

When listing an item on eBay, a seller can choose the listing format to be Auction-Style, Fixed Price, or eBay Store inventory. Sellers can also choose other options that will create optional formats.

The standard formats are as follows:

- **Auction-Style:** This is the most common format. Buyers place bids on an item and the highest bid wins.

- **Fixed Price:** This listing format is not an auction and there are no bids. The item is for sale at one stated price.

- **Store Inventory:** This lists the seller's item in her eBay Store at a fixed price.

The optional formats are as follows:

- **Private Auction:** Buyers' User IDs are hidden from view in the bid history list. It is used mostly in higher-price auctions.

SEE ALSO **4.29 "What is a Private Auction?"**

- **Auction-Style with Reserve:** The seller adds a minimum reserve price, which must at least be met during the bidding, or the item will not be sold.

- **Auction-Style with Buy It Now:** Enables buyers to either bid on an item or purchase the item at the stated price.

- **Auction-Style with Reserve and Buy It Now:** Same as above but also adds a minimum reserve price that must be met.

- **Multiple Item (Dutch) Auction:** Used to move several quantities of the same item, to one or more bidders, using the auction format.

- **Multiple Item Fixed Price Listing:** Used to sell quantities of product using the Fixed Price format.

- **Best Offer:** Buyers are allowed to make their best offer for the item rather than pay the listed Buy It Now price.

- **Classified Ad:** Allows sellers to advertise an item on eBay for a fee. No bidding takes place. Contact information is shared between the trading partners.

4.25 "Which selling format do you use?"

It depends on my reason for selling the item. If it is a new item that I have never sold before, I conduct research to determine how the top sellers are selling the item. I then use the research data to determine the best way to sell that item.

If it is part of my product line, then 90 percent of the time, I sell the item at a fixed price. The reason is that eBay selling is my business. I do not want my profits to be based on how well the auctions did that week. I need to make my profit margin for the item or I do not want to sell it. If the item doesn't sell, I will relist it again and sell it later.

SEE ALSO **4.34 "How should I conduct eBay research?"**

4.26 "When should I use an Auction-Style, Fixed Price, or Reserve listing?"

The brief answer is that your research will tell you which format to use based on what the top sellers of that particular item are using.

I mostly use Fixed Price listings when I sell items that appeal to men. Men are more inclined to buy quickly without a lot of shopping. They tend to shop online just like they shop at the mall. "Yes, that is the right price, shipping rate looks good, seller's feedback looks good. Okay, I want to Buy It Now and not have to wait to see if I win an auction."

I do list a few men's items Auction-Style because some men prefer this method. Women usually favor the auction format and they are often shopping for gifts for their boyfriends, brothers, husbands, sons, and fathers.

EBay sellers who sell items that appeal to women should primarily use 7-day auctions. Women tend to be better shoppers, have more patience, and enjoy winning the auction more than men, and therefore prefer Auction-Style rather than Fixed Price. However, you also need to realize that men are buying your items for their girlfriends, wives, sisters, and mothers. So you should also have some items that include the "Buy It Now" option for your male customers.

Am I generalizing or stereotyping here? Yes, but it is more appropriately called market research. You need to understand your customers and pay attention to bidding motivation and psychology.

Many PowerSellers who sell items that appeal to women change their listings from Auction-Style to Fixed Price during the Christmas season. It seems during that time, everyone is a power shopper.

I use a reserve price sparingly because it discourages bidders. I usually use it under three circumstances:

1. If my research has told me that the market is not consistent for this item and therefore I cannot be reasonably assured of what the final value of the auction will be.

2. If I have a valuable item and need to protect my investment.

3. If the item is very rare and I cannot find any research data for the item.

4.27 "What is the difference between a Buy It Now and a Fixed Price listing?"

When a seller lists a Fixed Price listing, there is no option to the buyer except to buy it or leave it (or sometimes make a Best Offer). A Buy It Now button can be added to an Auction-Style listing, allowing the buyer an option to either place a bid or forget the auction and just buy it immediately.

Note that when you create a Fixed Price listing, the button that appears on your listing will not say Fixed Price but rather Buy It Now. I think that is where the confusion comes from.

4.28 "Do you reveal what your reserve price is?"

No, but I sometimes give a very good hint. For example, if the item I am selling is worth $300 retail (MSRP) and my reserve is $100, I would write in my description that the reserve is around one third of MSRP.

Should you reveal your reserve? Do your research and see what the top sellers of the items in your category are doing. It is your decision.

I sometimes use a reserve in my auctions in order to keep the Buy It Now option "tease" available a few days longer. I set the reserve at what I call the tipping point. If a buyer is willing to bid a certain amount on the item, then he might as well go ahead and Buy It Now rather than lose the item to another buyer. You will need to experiment to find where the tipping point is for each of your items.

4.29 "What is a Private Auction?"

This option is sometimes selected by a seller when listing expensive items when he believes that the bidders may want to be more discreet or anonymous to everyone but the seller. With standard listings, eBay uses User ID masking so other bidders cannot determine or contact their competitors. For example, a bidder with the User ID of "moose" would appear as "m***e." A Private Auction causes the User IDs of the bidders to also be hidden from view on the closed auction page.

A seller may also choose this to keep other sellers from contacting her bidders. However, surveys reveal that 67 percent of buyers will skip over a private auction because they don't know what it means and tend to be suspicious.

Feedback

4.30 "Should I wait until I receive good feedback from my buyer to leave her feedback?"

If everyone waited for his trading partner to act first, no feedback would be left. As a buyer, I would wait until I received the item. You can't accurately rate the Detailed Seller Ratings for the seller until you have received the item. Was it described properly in the listing, packed professionally, and shipped promptly? If yes, the seller has earned my positive feedback. As a seller, think about it for a minute. You have a buyer who doesn't know you but has decided to put her trust in you, placed a winning bid on your item, and then paid you. You have her money in your hand (or PayPal account). What more do you need? She has fulfilled her obligation to you. You should leave positive feedback immediately after you receive her payment. Leaving prompt feedback for her will even encourage her to leave you positive feedback, provided you also pack and ship promptly.

4.31 "I am just getting started and I have zero (or very few) feedback(s). Is this going to hurt my sales?"

Not necessarily. The best way to get around this problem is to make sure your listings look professional. Many buyers are also new to eBay and may not even notice you have low feedback if your listings look like you know what you are doing.

It seems that the magic number is about 10 feedbacks. Once you have attained 10 feedbacks with a perfect score (100 percent positive), you now have a track record and buyers will begin to feel comfortable placing a bid on your item.

POWERSELLER TIP

Here's another tip to get your Feedback Score up quickly. Your total Feedback Score includes both selling and buying. Therefore, you may want to make your first dozen transactions on eBay inexpensive purchases from different PowerSellers. If you pay promptly with PayPal, you should receive positive feedback from the sellers. Many buyers will not even notice that all your feedback was from sellers. They will just see your Feedback Score is 12, and 100 percent positive.

Start by selling something simple like a used book. Create a great listing with your description, photo, and policies. The more professional your listings look, the less your number of feedbacks will matter.

4.32 "Should I send my buyer an e-mail and remind him to leave me feedback?"

Sure. I sometimes do that. Many times the buyer has just forgotten to leave the feedback. I would send him a very friendly feedback reminder e-mail—once. If he still doesn't respond, let it go. If you keep sending e-mails about feedback that he does not intend to leave, you will aggravate him. Remember that your feedback rating is in his hands. If you aggravate him, he may leave you feedback that you don't want. It is better to get no feedback than bad feedback. So ask once, then let it go.

4.33 "Why can't I leave negative feedback for my buyer?"

EBay changed this policy because some sellers were holding back their positive feedback until the buyer left positive feedback for them first. If the buyer left a negative feedback, the seller reciprocated with a negative even when the buyer didn't deserve it. In short, it was feedback extortion. Many buyers felt they could not leave an honest assessment because of the fear of retaliation from the seller. So the theory is that more honest assessments will be made by buyers under the new policy.

Sellers can still leave negative comments and report nonpaying buyers. EBay will remove any feedback left from the nonpaying buyer. A seller can also report any buyer who violates eBay policies and threatens negative feedback unless unreasonable demands are met. Additionally, after one year, eBay will remove any negative or neutral feedback from your overall percentage.

Conducting eBay Research

4.34 "How should I conduct eBay research?"

EBay sellers list any and all types of items. No one can be an expert on every item or category. Therefore, the purpose of your conducting research on eBay is to study how the top sellers (those with the best-performing listings) create their listings of the item you are about to sell. If you study how they list their items, you have eliminated the guesswork and will have a much better idea how to list your item. This step alone is often the difference between a successful listing and no or few bids.

Following are the steps to conduct research on eBay:

1. Login to your eBay account.

2. Click on the **Advanced Search** link.

3. Inside the **Enter Keyword or Item Number** box, type the keywords that you would use as a buyer to find the item you are about to list and click **Search.**

4. You will now see a list of all items currently for sale on eBay that include those keywords in their title. Narrow the list down to the specific item (if you can) by adding more keywords.

5. Once you have it narrowed to the specific item, you will see all the items currently for sale on eBay that match those keywords. Scroll down the left side, click the checkbox **Completed Listings,** and click **Search.**

6. Now you will see all the items that match the keywords for your item that have completed (ended) on eBay during the last two weeks. The prices in "green" mean those items sold for that price. The prices in "red" mean those items did not sell. Toward the top of the screen, click on the drop-down box and select **Price: Highest First.**

7. You now have a list of all items that have received the highest bids for the item you are about to sell.

Theoretically, you now have the top sellers of your item (those with the most successful price results). Be sure to exclude any outliers that may provide an artificially high price. For example, a seller may provide more than one item (or a bonus price, free shipping, and so on) in the listing. They would most likely end at a higher price and skew your results. Open the top 10 or more listings (only the ones with *green* prices, meaning they sold) and study how the top sellers listed the item. Look for the most important elements of success such as these:

- What were the keywords they used?
- In what category did they list the item?
- What was their starting bid?
- Did they use a reserve price?
- Was it an Auction-Style or Fixed Price listing?
- Did they use Buy It Now?
- How detailed was their description?
- How many photos did they use?
- How many days did they run their auction?
- How many hits did their auction attract?
- What day of the week and time did the listing end?

Write all this information down on a notepad for the top 10 (or more) sellers. Now you have some basic research to study that will help you create a successful listing for that particular item. Study the information and then merge and purge the outliers. If most sellers list the item as Auction-Style, then list your item as Auction-Style. If most sellers have a starting price under $10, then your starting price should be under $10.

Note that there are software companies that provide eBay research tools that can do all the search steps listed above plus provide detailed statistics about the item of interest. They provide all this information at your fingertips in just a few seconds.

The one I use most and highly recommend is HammerTap. All you do is enter the keywords for the item you are researching, and in about 10 seconds, it will provide all the research data you need.

4.35 "When I am conducting my eBay research, I can't find the item I want to sell. What do I do now?"

This is quite common. Searching for items using the **Completed listings only** check box will only reveal items that completed within the last 14 days. There is always a good chance that an item exactly like yours has not sold on eBay in the past two weeks. What I recommend is to do research elsewhere. If your item is just a standard item (not a collectible), I recommend you search for your item on the following websites in this order:

- www.amazon.com
- www.shopping.yahoo.com
- www.shopping.com
- www.froogle.com
- www.pricegrabber.com
- www.overstock.com

If you find your item in the preceding sites, subtract about 10–15 percent from their average selling price and that is probably what it will sell for on eBay.

For antiques and collectibles, you may also want to check these sites:

- www.goantiques.com
- www.tias.com

For more rare or collectible items it may take more work. If you still do not find your item from the sites above, I suggest you perform Yahoo!, MSN, Google, or other Internet searches for your item. If it is a rare or highly collectible item, search for online dealers or hobbyist, collector, and club sites that discuss the type of item you want to sell. Review their websites for an item similar to yours or a list of other sites that they recommend.

POWERSELLER TIP

If you are going to specialize in antique and collectible categories, I recommend joining Price Miner at www.priceminer.com. Their data contains items that date back several months for eBay and several years for www.goantiques.com and www.tias.com items. The results are then aggregated to offer you a complete guide. You can then sort by price, date, and other criteria.

Remember also that if your item is quite rare or there is no known market for it on eBay, be sure to protect yourself with a reserve price.

Otherwise, there may be only one bidder and the item sells for the starting bid.

4.36   "How can I find out what is hot on eBay?"

For a quick glance of the most popular items, go to the eBay homepage, select **Buy,** then **Popular Products** (toward the bottom of the page). Also, select the **Popular Searches** link.

For more specific searches such as the items that are hot in the categories where you sell, go to the Site Map and select **Seller Central,** then click the **What's Hot** link. This will give you a few ideas of products that the eBay merchandising team thinks will be hot sellers.

However, remember that what is hot on eBay is not always what is profitable. Hot items usually have many sellers and therefore high competition, resulting in low profit.

POWERSELLER TIP

If you want an excellent source of hot tips for products that will be hot *and* profitable, I use www.whatdoisell.com/studentrate. Lisa is an eBay trending expert. She has an excellent track record for finding the next "hot" items on eBay. With her information, you are always ahead of the curve and your competition.

4.37   "What are the biggest mistakes eBay sellers make?"

First of all, not conducting research before they list their item. They simply guess at everything and make hasty decisions. This produces hit-or-miss results. In short, they gamble.

Second, purchasing items to sell because they are "cheap" without doing their research on eBay first to be assured of a profit. Just because an item is cheap does not mean you can sell it for a profit on eBay. Therefore, I do my research first to guarantee the item is profitable on eBay *before* I purchase it to sell.

The operative word here is research. Learn how to conduct research before you purchase your items and before you list items. Research is the difference between professional and amateur sellers and, more important, between successful and unsuccessful listing results.

4.38 "Can I bid on my own item listings?"

No. This is prohibited for obvious reasons. EBay's software will not allow it to occur and will even block the transaction if you are bidding under your second User ID. Note that if you try this your account will be immediately suspended.

SEE ALSO **1.15 "My account was suspended on eBay. What happened?"**

4.39 "Can I have a friend or relative bid on my listings?"

The short answer is "no" if it is in auction format—even if your friend truly wants to purchase the item. He can, however, purchase your Buy It Now, Fixed Price listings.

Never have your friends bid on an item just to run up the current bid value for you. Please don't be tempted to do this. It is called shill bidding or simply "shilling," and is a very serious and unlawful offense.

EBay has very sophisticated software that looks for this type of activity. If you are caught, you are not only in trouble with eBay, but depending on the offense, they may report you to the attorney general of your state.

SEE ALSO **3.6 "What is shill bidding?"**

Advanced Listing Techniques

4.40 "How do I know how much to charge for shipping?"

See the answer to question 9.22 in Chapter 9.

4.41 "Can I list my item in two categories?"

Yes, but you will be charged double the Insertion Fee for your listing (but not double your Final Value Fee). The listing will still be for one item, but it will appear in two separate categories. Because you will be charged double fees, unless your item is expensive or sells equally well in both categories (based on your research), it is best to determine what category the top sellers are using and sell only in that category.

4.42 "I am selling an item that is a copy of, or looks like, a brand-name item. Can I call it Hummel-like or Gucci-style?"

Not in the title keywords. You cannot use the brand name of a similar item for your keywords if it is not indeed the brand's authentic item. However, you are allowed to use these types of descriptive phrases in the listing's description. Note that eBay is very clear that you cannot sell knock-offs of any item. For more information, select **Help,** type **keyword spam** in the search box, select **Keyword Spam Policy,** and then **Some Examples.**

4.43 "I have heard you can list items for longer than 10 days. How can I do that?"

Standard Auction-Style listings can last 1, 3, 5, 7, or 10 days. Store inventory and Fixed Price listings are available for 30 days.

4.44 "Why would anyone ever use a one-day auction?"

For two main reasons. One is if you have a time-sensitive item such as baseball playoff tickets that need to move *now!* Another reason would be if you are selling in a category that is so saturated that your item doesn't show up on the first few pages of a category until the last few hours or minutes of the auction. Your items are always lost among the crowd.

An example would be Christmas ornaments about the first week of December. Sellers may then choose to use one-day auctions so their items are always near the top of the category pages for those buyers just window-shopping through the category.

4.45 "When is the best day and time to start (and/or end) an auction?"

The consensus among eBay PowerSellers is that they receive the most, and highest, bids when they end their auctions on Sunday night between 5:00 P.M. and 7:00 P.M. PST. This makes sense when you realize that the vast majority of customers will be home and have access to their computer between those hours. This provides the maximum chance for your bidders to participate in all those last-minute bids that drive your final price higher. However, this recommended day and time is only a good rule of thumb. You need to keep in mind who your customers are.

If your customers tend to be business people who are surfing eBay while at work, ending them during the workday may make more sense. The same is true if your customers are stay-at-home moms. They may still be busy on Sunday nights, but may have more free time on Monday or Tuesday afternoons to surf eBay looking for your items.

Keep in mind your international customers as well. For several months I sold Marine Electronic Fish Finders. I had several customers in Australia. Therefore, I ran two separate auctions for those units. One auction would end on Sunday night at 7:00 P.M. PST for my North American customers, and one auction would end Sunday night at 7:00 P.M. Sydney time.

Starting and stopping your listings at specific dates and times are most important when your listings are in Auction-Style format. They are much less important when your listings are Fixed Price, as they can end at any time.

I suggest you start with Sunday night and then experiment from there for your own customers. There are also data-gathering and analysis tools that you can subscribe to that provide you with the best time and day to end a listing for the specific item you want to sell. The one I use and recommend again is HammerTap.

4.46 "How can I get my listing to kick off at a certain date and time?"

Scheduled listing is a great feature that eBay provides for sellers and an important component to your listing's success. It enables you to create the listing whenever you have the time, but have it become active on eBay at a time and date up to three weeks into the future.

For example, you want an auction to begin on a Sunday night at 6:00 P.M. but will not be available at that time to create the listing. You can instead create the listing at any time earlier in the week and use a drop-down menu on the Selling Format Page to select the date and time that you want the auction to begin. EBay charges 10¢ for this feature.

4.47 "Are there particular days or times I should avoid having my auction end?"

Several factors can affect a listing that are outside the realm of eBay. Some of the times that are generally considered unsuitable for ending eBay auctions are these:

- Major holidays (except Thanksgiving)
- Tax season
- Friday nights and, to a lesser extent, Wednesday
- Any auction that ends in the middle of the night
- Major sporting events such as the Super Bowl
- Summer, especially July, because so many are on vacation

The week of the Fourth of July has historically been the worst week of the year for my sales. It is a tough time for Auction-Style listings because many potential buyers are on vacation. This leads to a much lower final price.

A few years ago I stopped selling Auction-Style listings and only sold Fixed Price listings during July. This seemed to work for my most popular items. So I now give the rest of my items the summer off. A twist to this theory is that the summer is a great time to buy on eBay!

Finally, remember that the days mentioned above are only suggestions. Every product is different and you may even find that a Friday or a Wednesday is a great time to sell your particular items. Use eBay research and your own Sales Reports to help analyze your own data.

SEE ALSO **5.9 "What metrics do you use for your eBay business?"**

4.48 "I have a large quantity of a particular item. How many can I sell on eBay at the same time?"

When selling identical items, one at a time, using the Auction-Style format, you can only have 15 separate listings on eBay at the same time. For example, say you have 50 iPods that are the same color and model. You can only have 15 separate listings. When a few sell, you can list more as long as you do not exceed 15. If you have the same model but in a different color, you can have 15 additional listings of that color. If you have multiple User IDs, you still can only have a total of 15 listings at the same time. Remember that you can sell with no limitations of product quantity using a Fixed Price listing. You can also have "choice" listings where you give the buyer a choice of color or size. However, you would be limited to 15 of those listings, each with multiple quantities (Fixed Price) or choices (Auction-Style or Fixed Price) of product.

4.49 "When I list several items that are the same on eBay, should I list them all at once or spread them out?"

If you list 15 of the same product (model and color), then yes, I would probably spread them out a bit. The time gap depends on the popularity of the category. If you list them 15 minutes apart, but the category is sluggish, they will still all be listed together. If it is a popular category, separating the listings by 15–30 minutes may spread them out enough that there will be other items in between yours.

If the item you are selling is Fixed Price, it is less important to start or end the listing at a certain time. Whenever it sells, the ending time is immediate. Therefore, if you are listing the same items as Fixed Price, consider separating them by several hours or even days.

If you are listing several of your items as Auction-Style but they are not all the same item, then it does not matter if they are all listed together. It is more important that they end on Sunday night between 5:00–7:00 P.M. PST (as a general rule), than it is to spread them out past those times just to separate your items.

4.50 "I have an item listed on eBay, but I notice that it has an error in it. Can I correct the error?"

You can correct errors to your listing, as long as there have been no bids on the item or if the item is not about to expire within the next 12 hours. This is a great reason to double-check all your listings before you upload them to eBay. The fastest I have sold an item was three minutes! So double check your listings before you submit them and then immediately after they appear on eBay.

Here's how to revise your auction:

1. Go to your my eBay page, select your **Active** selling link, and select the listing you need to correct.

2. Toward the top left in the Seller Status box, click on **Revise your item.** Sometimes eBay will ask you to login again to verify that you are indeed the seller.

3. Scrolling down the right side, you will see edit links for each section. Select the link that is pertinent to the section in which revision is needed (such as "edit title, subtitle, & categories," "edit description," "edit pictures & details," "add payment options," and so on).

Note that if the area you want to edit is not available to edit (no link provided), then either there are bids on your item or your listing is about to expire. If that is the case, sorry, you cannot revise that portion of your listing, but you can amend it. If there are bids on the item, eBay allows you a link where you can amend the description, which places your revisions at the bottom of the auction for buyers to see.

Seller Fees

4.51 "What types of fees are charged to the seller?"

There are three types of fees on eBay for standard listings:

- **Insertion Fee:** The first fee associated with an eBay listing and is directly related to the starting price.

- **Final Value Fee:** Charged only if your item sells and the fee is only applied to the item's final bid value. The shipping rate is not included in determining the Final Value Fee.

- **Listing Upgrade Fees:** Charged for nonstandard, optional formats or enhancements to eBay listings. More advanced sellers may use these enhancements as strategies to increase the item's visibility, hopefully resulting in more hits, bids, and ultimately a higher final price for the item.

You can find the current fees by selecting the **Help** link at the top of the homepage and typing **fees** in the search field. For Listing

Upgrade Fees, type **upgrade fees** in the search field, select **ebay.com fees,** and then scroll down to **Listing Upgrade Fees** and click the arrow next to the text.

4.52 "Where can I find or determine the eBay seller fees for my account?"

Select the **Seller Account** link in your My eBay page under the My Account section. You can now view your invoices and fees.

4.53 "Can I charge a surcharge to offset my eBay or PayPal fees?"

No, this is against eBay policy. However, you should account for it when determining your starting or fixed price for the item.

Other Basic Seller Questions

4.54 "Can I cancel an auction if it is not going well?"

You can cancel an auction, but it should be for reasons other than "it is not going well." It should be because you made a mistake and the item is no longer for sale—such as if the item was lost or broken. Note that you will forfeit your Insertion Fees or Listing Upgrade Fees if you cancel a listing. Therefore, if it is not too late to revise your item, revision is a better choice.

SEE ALSO 4.50 "I have an item listed on eBay, but I notice that it has an error in it. Can I correct the error?"

Keep in mind that most of your bids will come in the last few hours, minutes, or seconds of an auction. An auction that is not doing well with two days to go has little bearing on how it will actually finish. You can get a good feel for how well the item will finish by checking your My eBay to see how many buyers are watching your item.

To cancel a listing, go to My eBay and use the drop-down menu next to the item in "Items I'm Selling" and select **End Item.**

EBay does keep track of these things. Canceling a Fixed Price listing is of no concern to eBay, as there have been no bids. However, canceling auctions once they are underway is not in the spirit of eBay. If you do it too often, you may be contacted by eBay.

4.55 "A potential buyer asked me to stop the auction early and sell the item off eBay. What should I do?"

This is absolutely forbidden by eBay. In some cases, these e-mails are fraud. Some are even generated from your competitors!

This practice is not in the spirit of auctions or fair to your other bidders. Send an e-mail stating that you are not allowed and will not do that, but wish him the best of luck in the auction. Keep your e-mail friendly in case the buyer is legitimate and just unaware of eBay rules. The recipient may decide to bid on your items now or in the future.

If there have been no bids, however, you can always add a Buy It Now price to the auction. Once you've added the price, you can contact the buyer about the new opportunity.

4.56 "Should I answer a customer's e-mail through eBay or directly to her e-mail address?"

Respond through eBay. If you respond directly to her e-mail address from your e-mail and she has a spam blocker active, your e-mail may never get to her. EBay's pass-through e-mail system guarantees delivery. I rarely answer an e-mail from my e-mail account because of all the spoof e-mails. I just answer the question through eBay. Keep it simple and safe.

Note that at the time of this writing, eBay has just announced a new system for e-mail forwarding. They will be masking all e-mail addresses, so when sellers select **reply**, it will generate an e-mail address mask that the seller will see. The seller will then auto-forward the e-mail to the buyer. That way sellers will not be able to capture e-mail addresses of users that have not won one of their items.

4.57 "I have heard sellers say we need to turn on our Baydar. What is that?"

The meaning of Baydar (eBay Radar) is simply that as an eBay seller you need to always be looking for new products, tools, hints, and tips to help you in your eBay business. Specifically, you should be on the lookout for new products that may be a success on eBay.

When you shop at stores that you frequent, most likely you go down the same aisles picking up the same products. What I suggest that you do next time is to stroll aisles, departments, and stores that you do not frequent. Review items on the shelves looking for products that you did not even know existed or had never thought about selling.

Do the same thing when scanning magazines and especially the Sunday paper. Don't skip over the ads; study them. What new products have you found? Then do your research on eBay to see how they are selling. Can you make a profit? Contact the manufacturer to find the wholesaler for your area. That is turning on your "Baydar!" Note that this entire process is detailed in my book, *eBay Rescue Profit Maker* (Alpha Books, 2009).

4.58 "I would like to sell a car (or several cars) on eBay. How do I do that?"

The answer to this question could be another book in itself. In some states, you need a car dealer's license to sell more than just one car a year. I recommend you visit eBay Motors and do a lot of reading and research before you list a car (or buy one) on eBay. For this information, see the following links:

- http://pages.motors.ebay.com/howto/overview.html
- Kelly's Blue Book is available at www.kbb.com.

Keep a few things in mind when selling cars. First, don't make a car your first listing on eBay. Learn the eBay listing creation process and make your mistakes on simple, inexpensive items. Second, take multiple pictures from numerous angles both inside and outside of the car. Third, be sure to mention any and all positive features as well as any flaws. The buyer should have no surprises when he takes possession.

I personally wouldn't recommend attempting to sell a car on eBay until you have had at least two or three dozen transactions. You need the experience as well as the confidence to do it right. Use your research to study other eBay Motors sellers very closely, for some time, and you will get it right. I would also suggest you consider using an escrow service such as www.escrow.com to handle the financial transaction.

If you still don't feel comfortable, go to www.ebay.com/ta and hire a professional Trading Assistant. Make sure they specialize in selling autos. You also need to check them out thoroughly and understand their terms.

SEE ALSO   **4.60** "Is there someone who can sell my items on eBay for me?"

4.59   "How should I sell a large number of inherited or estate items?"

Depending on the volume of items to liquidate, you may have a nearly overwhelming task for a new eBay seller. How many items are we talking about? Is it less than 300 or more like 1,000? If less than 300, you can probably manage it yourself selling one at a time on eBay.

If it's too many items and it's overwhelming, I suggest you separate the items by value (do your research on eBay to determine the value), then do the following:

- Throw away or give away items that will bring in little or no money on eBay.

- If an item is in good condition but probably worth under $30, consider donating it to charity.

- Give all items of significant value (like an old Steinway piano) to a true professional Trading Assistant or an estate liquidation service and pay them to handle those items.

- If the number of remaining items is still overwhelming then give any item worth about $500 or more to the Trading Assistant as well.

- Now you can sell all the other lower-priced items yourself.

4.60   "Is there someone who can sell my items on eBay for me?"

Yes. They are called Trading Assistants (TAs). All you have to do is drop off your item at their place of business and they will handle everything from there. They will do the research, take the pictures, write the description, submit the listing, answer customer's questions, and pack and ship the item for you. They will collect the money, take their percentage, and give you the majority. If the item doesn't sell, they will return it to you.

TAs usually charge a fee of about 35–40 percent, but keep in mind that about 10 percent of that is taken by eBay and PayPal fees, so their net is 25 percent for doing everything. It is a good arrangement because they do all the work.

Be sure you ask how long they have been doing this and exactly what they charge (including whether eBay and PayPal fees are included in their commission), and check their site and feedback before you decide which one to use. You want an experienced professional, not someone who does this as a hobby. Note also that TAs who meet certain guidelines and have a physical store with regular hours are called Registered eBay Drop-Off Locations (REDOL). You should check if a REDOL is in your area as well. To find eBay Trading Assistants and REDOL near you, go to www.ebay.com/ta.

SEE ALSO   5.12 "How can I learn about becoming a Trading Assistant?"

4.61   "How long do I have before I have to ship an item that I sold?"

Sellers are required to ship the item within 15 days of the auction ending date. However, buyers can issue an Item not Received report after 10 days. Because UPS and Parcel Post can take a week to travel coast to coast, I recommend that you ship your item as soon as possible (one to two days) after the auction ends. This will also help your chances of receiving positive Detailed Seller Ratings (DSR) Feedback Scores.

4.62   "Can I sell anything on eBay?"

No. In fact, several items are either restricted or outright prohibited on eBay. Think alcohol, tobacco, and firearms (ATF). These items are prohibited. However, items related to them may be restricted or even allowed.

For example, you can't sell tobacco but you can sell all related accessories such as lighters and cigar humidors. You can't sell wine, but the exception is if the wine is considered a collectible, then it's more valuable than the retail value.

If you are considering selling any item that is related to ATF or could cause harm, you need to be sure the item is allowed on eBay. Also, be aware that many other items such as knock-offs are prohibited. Other items may be allowed but are restricted in how they can be sold. If you have any doubts, check eBay first by selecting **Help** and typing **Prohibited Items**. If you cannot get a clear answer, select the **Live help** link and ask a live eBay representative.

4.63   "Can I sell recalled items on eBay?"

No, and it is your responsibility to ensure that your items have not been recalled. This also applies to recalled used items. The list of recalled items from the U.S. Consumer Product Safety Commission is very large. To be sure your item is not recalled, go to www.cpsc.gov/cpscpub/prerel/prerel.html.

4.64   "I see sellers who are selling prohibited items or are doing something that violates eBay rules. Why can they get away with it?"

Just because you see a speeding driver zoom past you on the freeway doesn't make it okay for you to speed. These eBay violators will eventually get caught if they continue with the prohibited practice or violation. If it is a serious violation, report them using the **Report This Item** link at the bottom of the listing page.

4.65   "I have an item that I've listed several times and it just won't sell. What should I do?"

Many factors may cause that to happen. Use the checklist that follows to try to determine the problem. Also review question 4.68 to ensure that you have created a great listing.

❏   When you conducted research, did you confirm that there was demand on eBay for the product?

SEE ALSO **4.34** "How should I conduct eBay research?"

❏ Did you also conduct your eBay research to determine how to sell the item before you created the listing?

❏ How many hits did you get?

If fewer than 10 hits, buyers can't find you. Check your keywords, the spelling of your keywords, and category.

SEE ALSO **4.18** "What are your suggestions for writing a great title?"

If more than 50 hits, buyers can find you, but they aren't taking the bait. Check your starting price and shipping rate, or look for mistakes with your photos, or typos in the description.

If your hits are between 10 and 50, it is most likely another problem listed below.

❏ Is your starting price too high? EBay research will give you this answer.

❏ Is your shipping rate too high or shipping method unusual?

❏ Are you using a reserve price? If so, is it too high?

❏ Read your description carefully, looking for obvious mistakes that could be confusing.

SEE ALSO **4.1** "What is your advice for writing a good description?"

❏ Do you have an unusual or harsh tone in your shipping, payment, or return policies?

❏ Is there something wrong with a photo? Is it out of focus, or did you insert the wrong one?

❏ Have you made a mistake during listing creation such as listing the item as a private auction?

❏ Did you forget to end the listing on a Sunday night between 5 and 7 P.M. PST?

❏ Is the item seasonal and, if so, are you selling it in the off-season?

❏ Do you have a lot of competition? If yes, maybe there is more supply than demand. Maybe a new seller is dumping product. Let it rest temporarily in your eBay Store until the supply subsides.

❏ If there is no significant competition, maybe there is low demand with the current buyers on eBay. Let the item rest awhile and wait for new buyers to come into the marketplace. Maybe give it three or four weeks and then try again.

❏ Still didn't sell a month later? If you still are not receiving any bids, maybe there is no demand for it.

So you just can't sell that used 1977 clock radio with the broken knobs and scratchy volume control, eh? Unless it was "Star Wars themed," my bet is that the market demand is pretty thin for your old, trusty (or is that "rusty"?) radio. Here are your options:

• If it truly is in poor condition, throw it away.

• If it is still in good condition, combine it with other more valuable items or include it in an auction as a freebie.

• Garage-sale time.

• Donate it to charity (only if your item is in good working condition).

• Place it in a Bargain Bin category in your eBay Store and let it sit until it is sold.

• Wrap it up and give it to your brother-in-law on his birthday.

4.66 "Can I somehow discover what the highest bid amount is from my top bidder?"

No. That is between the bidder and eBay. Sellers are not allowed to see the actual highest bid initially placed because many would be tempted to shill. For a more detailed explanation, see the proxy and shill bidding questions in the "See Also" references that follow.

SEE ALSO 2.18 "Sometimes when I bid on an item, eBay immediately says I have been outbid. This seems suspicious to me. What is going on?"

SEE ALSO 3.6 "What is shill bidding?"

4.67 "How can I stay current with everything that is happening on eBay?"

I recommend that you spend some time browsing eBay's Seller Central available from the **Site Map** link. There are several sections in particular where you can keep up with the latest happenings for the categories where you sell.

Category Tips: This section keeps sellers informed of the changes that affect the categories in which they sell. Information is listed by categories to enable you to check for changes in your area of interest.

eBay Pulse: This segment offers a list of particular items that have been the most popular searches by prospective buyers. Go to http://pulse.ebay.com.

In Demand: This link in the Category Tips shows a list of the keywords that buyers have used for item searches and gives the top five eBay Stores with the most active listings for a particular category.

Discussion Boards: This is an opportunity to make contact with experienced sellers who have similar interests. You can search these discussion boards and read the information, comments, questions, and answers.

Announcement Boards: Lists all of the changes to eBay policies, procedures, and fees.

Newsletters: Ina Steiner provides a free newsletter that gives daily updates, news, happenings, and insights that revolve around eBay, online e-commerce, and other auction sites. You can subscribe at www.auctionbytes.com. I also provide a free eBay newsletter with buying and selling tips and strategies at my website www.trainingu4auctions.com.

WhatDoISell®: Every serious eBay seller needs to join this site. It offers the best product trending and analysis I have found for eBay and online sellers. Most eBay sellers source products that are on a downtrend such as garage and estate sales or liquidation items. With the information from WhatDoISell®, you will know what the coming trends are and can ride the wave of the entire product life cycle. You can become a member of her site at a substantial discount at www.whatdoisell.com/studentrate.

SEE ALSO **12.23** "How can I find reputable wholesales, liquidators, importers, and drop shippers?"

4.68 "What is the best advice you can give a new seller in order to have a successful listing?"

If you keep the following in mind, you will have the best chance for your listing to be successful and beat your competition.

- Conduct eBay marketplace research before you list any item. Believe your research results and list your item the same way that the top sellers do for that particular item. Likewise, one of the biggest mistakes that new sellers make is they conduct their research properly but then decide to list their item differently from what their research results suggest.

SEE ALSO **4.34** "How should I conduct eBay research?"

- Spend considerable time researching and then deciding on the right keywords. It is how 80 percent of your customers will find you. You only have 55 characters to work with, so use them wisely.

- Include alternative spellings of product names if applicable for your item. Check your keywords for misspellings.

- Possibly include intentionally misspelled keywords if buyers routinely misspell the item or brand name. Include the brand name keywords spelled correctly, as well as how they are commonly misspelled. For example, use Cuisinart and Cusinart. For help with this, go to www.typobid.com.

- Browsing categories is how the other 20 percent of your customers will find you. Therefore, use a professional-looking gallery picture and list your auction in the best category for your item (based again on your research). If all your competition is using the same photo from the manufacturer's website, take your own photo. Mix it up and maybe take a picture of the box instead of the item. Now *your* listing is the one that stands out from all the others.

- Charge a reasonable shipping rate. You do not want to lose the sale because of excessive shipping charges. Buyers avoid shipping gougers like the plague. They can also give poor Detailed Seller Ratings feedback about your shipping rates.

- Learn to take professional-looking photos. Your gallery picture is one of the most important differentiating factors between you and your competition, assuming all other factors (price, shipping rate, etc.) are equal.

- Think like a buyer when you write your description. Answer the questions she will have about the item such as what the item is, what the auction includes, the condition of the item, your shipping rates, and return policies.

  Use the fonts, type sizes, and layout that buyers are used to reading in books, magazines, or newspapers.

  Use proper grammar, punctuation, and syntax.

  Never use ALL CAPS (all capital letters) for body text. It is too difficult to read. Use Mixed Case.

  Use only black and white for the description text. A headline that is in color may be suitable in limited use but not for text.

  Avoid using colored backgrounds because it often conflicts with the text, making it hard to read.

  Describe the item accurately and honestly.

  Use spell-check to ensure your description has no misspellings.

- Always complete the Item Specifics if they are offered for your item.

- For more technical equipment, also include make, manufacturer, model number, technical specifications, and warranty status. You can usually get technical specs from the manufacturer's website.

- Schedule your listing to end on the best day and time for your item. This is usually on weekend evenings for general items.

SEE ALSO **4.45 "When is the best day and time to start (and/or end) an auction?"**

5 Advanced Selling

For many sellers, the momentum of eBay keeps building. Throughout my involvement with eBay instruction, I have seen a noticeable pattern of questions as my students progress in experience and sales.

Nonpaying and Troublemaking Bidders

5.1 "How should I handle a winning bidder who hasn't paid for the item and won't respond to my e-mails?"

In most cases, the buyer is either 1) away from her computer and doesn't even realize she won the auction, 2) she thought she had already paid, or 3) she has forgotten. I have even had some customers who were in the hospital.

Give her the benefit of the doubt, send a payment-reminder e-mail, and allow another three days for a response. If she doesn't respond, send her one more reminder e-mail with a 24-hour deadline to pay.

If you still do not hear from her, you may want to call her. Select the **Advanced Search** link, then **Find a Member,** and enter the member's User ID. EBay will e-mail you her phone number. However, note that they will also e-mail your phone number to your customer as well. Keep your conversation professional, friendly, and nonthreatening. Just remind her that her time to pay for the item has passed and she needs to pay immediately.

If the buyer refuses to pay or if you do not hear from her, it is time to get your eBay fees back. If she does not agree to cancel the transaction, then you need to report her as a nonpaying bidder. See the next question.

POWERSELLER TIP

> If you want to avoid the hassle with a nonpaying customer, consider making an offer to cancel the transaction. Sometimes she will accept this and then you can close the transaction, avoid further problems, and get your fees back. See question 5.3.

5.2   "How do I report a nonpaying bidder so I can get my eBay fees returned?"

If all attempts have been exhausted and the buyer will not pay or respond to your e-mails for at least seven days, it is time to report the nonpaying bidder in order to get your fees back. An Unpaid Item on eBay is known as a UPI. Select the **Help** link and type **unpaid item process.** Here, you can read the details about the dispute process.

To file the dispute, go to your My eBay account and select **Dispute Console,** then **Report an Unpaid Item,** and enter the item number. Select **The buyer has not paid for the item** and follow all online directions from there.

Once you have filed an official dispute, eBay will remind the buyer about your UPI claim with a pop-up message every time she logs in to eBay for 14 days. This usually kick-starts her into action to either pay or contact you. If it doesn't, let it run for seven days and then return to the Dispute Console to request that your Final Value Fees be returned.

Note that this UPI will be on the nonpaying bidder's record as strike one. If she receives three UPI strikes, then, just like in baseball, she is "out" of eBay. This is a good way for sellers to police, clean up, or get rid of deadbeat buyers.

If you need further help with this process, go to eBay's homepage and select **Live help.** A chat window will open and you can communicate with a live eBay representative.

5.3   "The winning bidder has buyer's remorse and wants to cancel the transaction. What should I do?"

When a buyer makes this request, I always agree to cancel the transaction. My decision is based on my customer service policy. I always offer a money-back guarantee. Therefore, I actually appreciate the fact that he asked to cancel the transaction before I shipped the item. I simply cancel the transaction and then make the item available to the second-highest bidder with a Second Chance Offer.

SEE ALSO **3.13 "What is a Second Chance Offer?"**

If you agree to cancel the transaction, then eBay needs to be notified. EBay has charged you a Final Value Fee for the item and assumes you were paid. You need to file the proper online forms to have your fees refunded.

1. Go to your My eBay.

2. Select the **Dispute Console** link.

3. Select **Report an Unpaid Item.**

4. Enter the item number.

5. For the reason of cancellation, select **We have both agreed not to complete the transaction.**

6. Answer the questions and follow the directions from there.

EBay will send a confirmation e-mail to the buyer. Once he responds to eBay that he agrees with the cancellation, the Final Value Fees will be credited to your account.

5.4 "How can I block a difficult or nonpaying buyer from bidding on my items in the future?"

It is a good idea to block a nonpaying bidder from placing bids on any of your items in the future. I also block buyers who are being unreasonable or have caused me any trouble during a transaction. I don't want to ever have to deal with them again so I block them from my future listings.

Here's how to block a buyer:

1. Login to eBay.

2. Select **Site Map.**

3. Scroll down to the Selling Activities section.

4. Select **Block Bidding/Buyer List.**

5. Select **Add an eBay user to My Blocked Bidder/Buyer List.**

6. Enter the buyer's User ID in the box provided (I prefer to list each User ID separately on a new line).

POWERSELLER TIP

Each quarter I conduct product research on my competition. I look for new items that I may want to add to my product line. I also look to see if my competitors have received any negative feedback in the last three months. If they have, I click on that listing and find who left the negative feedback. I then read several of the feedback comments they have left for sellers. If I see a pattern of bad comments, I have identified a troublemaker. I then add that buyer's User ID to my blocked list. Because they buy items in the same category where I sell, I just eliminated a potential troublemaker.

5.5 "How can I prevent other potential problem buyers from bidding on my items?"

EBay's Buyer Requirements tool enables sellers to automatically prevent or limit buyers from bidding on or buying their items if certain criteria have not been met. The criteria include the following:

- Buyer is registered in a country where the seller doesn't want to ship.

- Buyer has a negative Feedback Score.

- Buyer has two or more recent Unpaid Item strikes.

- Buyer does not have a PayPal account.

Here's how to block a buyer who meets any of these criteria:

1. Select **Site Map,** then under Sell, select **Block Bidder/Buyer List.**

2. Click the **buyer blocks** link.

3. Place a check mark next to each reason you wish to block, and select the number of UPI strikes or policy violations. I suggest that you make each block based on the minimum number of violations within the maximum amount of time.

4. Check **Apply above settings to current and future listings** and click **Submit.**

Sales Metrics

5.6 "What is a good sell-through rate for an eBay seller?"

Sell-through percentage rates, sometimes confused with conversion rates, compare the number of items that were listed to the number of items that actually sold. The formula is "items sold" divided by "items listed" (sold ÷ listed). For example, if you listed 10 items and 7 sold (7 ÷ 10), you had a .7 or 70 percent sell-through rate.

It is important to keep an eye on your sell-through percentage rate for particular items. If you find that an item has a low sell-through percentage month after month, you need to reexamine your reason for selling that item. However, I think that sell-through rates are over-rated as a measurement of a seller's success. Profit margin is a much better measurement.

Some sellers seem obsessed with their sell-through rates and compare their rate to other sellers. They then wonder and worry what is wrong if their own score is lower. I have a sell-through rate that is about 60–90 percent depending on the products I sell. Those rates are quite acceptable and profitable for me.

Think about it for a moment. If I listed Rolex watches on eBay for a Fixed Price of $100, I guarantee you I would have a 100 percent sell-through rate. My business would also be bankrupt. If, however, I listed Rolex watches with a reserve or fixed price that doubled my money, I could have a sell-through rate of 20 percent and still be selling enough watches to have a very healthy bottom line.

A sell-through percentage rate is a metric that you should track for your business, but it is much less relevant than other areas of your business. See the next three questions.

5.7 "What is the difference between a sell-through rate and a conversion rate?"

A sell-through rate compares the total number of listings placed by a seller to the number of listings that actually sell. A conversion rate compares the number of hits an eBay Store or website receives to the number of sales made. In short, it reveals how many shoppers you are converting to buyers.

5.8 "What do you consider a good profit margin?"

This is answered in question 13.6.

5.9 "What metrics do you use for your eBay business?"

I pay close attention to my profit margins and, to a lesser extent, my sell-through percentages. I don't use other hard metrics as much as just pay attention to certain areas of my business. The areas I watch closely are sales reports, expenses, product cost, profitability, and inventory turnover.

Sales Reports

You can subscribe to, or access, your eBay sales reports by going to your My eBay page and selecting the **Sales Reports** link under **Subscriptions.** The reports use tables and charts to provide a quick snapshot of your recent sales activities as well as a comparison of sales over a given period. The reports cover sales and fees.

Sales Reports Plus provides additional information including sales by format, category, ending day, ending time, Unpaid Item activity, duration, and your sales compared to an average of all sellers in your category. Both subscriptions are free!

Expenses

Keep your business expenses under control. Watch for sales on business equipment and supplies that you use. Do you really need a new $2,000 computer, or can you get by with one for $500?

Buy office supplies on eBay or from discount stores such as Costco and Sam's Club or online from www.uline.com. Shipping supplies can eat into your profits quickly. Therefore, as much as possible, use free or low-cost packing and shipping supplies.

SEE ALSO **9.11** "Do you also purchase your packing materials online?"

Watch your eBay fees. Do you really need all those extra pictures or listing upgrades? Listing enhancements can add up quickly. Try a test-listing without the frills and see if your sell-through rate for that item is the same. When doing a product test, be sure to change just one variable with each test. That way, you know that nothing else affected the result. Even better, let HammerTap provide this information for you without having to run trials.

SEE ALSO **5.26** "Which product-analysis tools do you use and recommend?"

Product Cost

Monitor the costs of your products closely. You know that gadget that your distributor sells to you for $15 and you sell on eBay for $27? Did you notice on that last invoice that your distributor raised the wholesale price from $15 to $25, while the MSRP stayed the same? Continuing to list the gadget at $27 is no longer profitable. Watch your product costs closely, drop items that are no longer profitable, replace them with new items that are, and take advantage of seasonal sales from your supplier.

Inventory Turnover

I use "just in time" inventory management for my eBay business. I do not keep large quantities of inventory. Instead, I watch my inventory stock closely. I understand thoroughly the average quantity of each item I sell each week, as well as the lead-time required from each of my suppliers. As soon as my inventory reaches my predetermined minimum supply, I place an order with my supplier in just enough time to resupply my stock before it sells out. So while my sold eBay items are moving out the front door with the USPS, my inventory re-supply is coming in the back door from UPS. I usually turn over my entire inventory at least once or sometimes twice a month.

In short, I do not stock large quantities of inventory that I won't even sell for several months. I save money by keeping my inventory stock low, moving products quickly, and coordinating sales with my re-supply. I can then use this money for other business purposes—such as purchasing more items to sell!

For maximum inventory budget efficiency, you need to carry many different items that turn over quickly. Use "just in time" inventory management so you can benefit from "broad and thin" inventory, not "narrow and deep."

PowerSellers and Trading Assistants

5.10 "What are the different PowerSeller levels?"

A PowerSeller is an eBay seller who has received at least 100 feedbacks and maintains a 98 percent positive feedback rating. She must also maintain a certain sales or volume level averaged over the last three months. The minimum monthly sales or volume (one or the other, not both) requirements for the five PowerSeller levels are as follows:

PowerSeller Minimum Monthly Sales or Volume Levels					
	Bronze	Silver	Gold	Platinum	Titanium
Sales	$1,000	$3,000	$10,000	$25,000	$150,000
Volume	100	300	1,000	2,500	15,000

There is also a provision for PowerSeller qualifications that involve seasonal sellers. Under this exception, a seller can also become a PowerSeller if they achieve sales of $12,000 or 1,200 items sold for the past 12 months.

5.11 "What level of PowerSeller would be a good goal to try to attain?"

Your level of PowerSeller is not nearly as relevant as the profitability and volume your business produces. Let's look at an example comparing two PowerSellers. First, note that a Bronze PowerSeller means she has at least 100 feedbacks and a 98 percent positive rating, and has maintained a minimum average of $1,000 per month for three months in eBay sales. A Silver PowerSeller must maintain the same level of feedback, as well as a minimum average of $3,000 in sales over the same period.

The first PowerSeller is selling individual beanie babies for $5 and makes a profit of $2 each. She needs to list, sell, pack, and ship 200 beanie babies a month to be a Bronze PowerSeller. That is a lot of work for the lowest-level status and only a $400 profit.

The second PowerSeller sells the latest marine electronics GPS navigation receivers for $1,000 with a profit of $200 each. She lists, sells, packs, and ships only two units per month, but her profit is also $400.

Both sellers are PowerSellers with about the same profit per month. However, the second seller has double the sales revenue, the same $400 profit, and, best of all, only 1 percent the amount of work.

You need to look at net profit and product volume, not gross sales. Remember, it takes just as long to list, pack, and ship a $1 profit item as it does a $100 profit item. That is a very powerful wake-up call and reminder to all eBay sellers.

I am not at all suggesting that you should be selling only higher-priced items on eBay. I am merely making the point that a certain PowerSeller level status is irrelevant to how successful and profitable your eBay business is or how busy you are. There is a saying among experienced eBay sellers that your goal should not be to become a PowerSeller, but rather a profit seller.

5.12 "How can I learn about becoming a Trading Assistant?"

A Trading Assistant (TA) is an eBay seller who lists other people's items on eBay on consignment. They handle all of the work involved including taking the pictures, creating the listing, answering customers questions, collecting the money, and shipping the item. Most TAs charge about 35 to 40 percent for their service.

Go to www.ebaytradingassistant.com. Be sure to read about Registered eBay Drop-Off Locations (REDOL). They are TAs who have a place of business and keep regular hours.

5.13 "What is your opinion of becoming a Trading Assistant or opening a Registered eBay Drop-Off Location?"

It is a tough business. Have you noticed that many of the eBay drop-off stores near you have closed? Many were managed by experienced eBay sellers but just couldn't make it work. That is a big clue.

Many customers who consider using this type of service tend to be people who don't want to pay others for something that they can do. Therefore, you will be haggling over your service fees. They also tend to have unrealistic expectations and can be difficult when their

Al Kaline autographed baseball sold for a lot less than they thought it should.

The type of customers who make this kind of business profitable are people who need to liquidate items quickly. This could be because of an inheritance of collectible items, a need to liquidate items quickly for emergency money, or because they are moving. You will need to determine how to market your skills and expertise to this narrow segment of customers.

It seems that the TAs who are profitable are no longer marketing to individuals but to businesses. In effect, they are a liquidation service for many local businesses. For example, what if you were able to get a contract with a rental car agency to liquidate used cars on eBay Motors? Use that example and scale it down to the particular businesses in your locality.

Website Linking

5.14   "I have a website. Can I link from my eBay listings to my website?"

Only if your website is used for informational purposes. You cannot link to any website that sells items. This is because eBay assumes you are just using them as advertising and then sending the buyers to your website where you don't have to pay the eBay fees. You can't use active or static links (i.e., you can't mention your website). You can, however, link to any of your active eBay listings, eBay Store, or your About Me page.

There is one exception to the link rules. You can link from your About Me page to your website as long as you don't show or mention any actual products in your About Me page.

EBay has several rules for their Links Policy. To learn more, select the **Help** link and type **Links Policy** in the search box. To specifically learn more about linking from your About Me page, go to http:// pages.ebay.com/help/feedback/about_me.html. Note that you can place links to your website in eBay's Classified Ad listing format (see question 5.16).

5.15 "Can I link from my website to my eBay listings?"

Absolutely! EBay would love you to send traffic to them. In fact, if you have an eBay Store, they will give you 75 percent off your Final Value Fee if the buyer, sent from your website, purchases any of your items (provided you enter the right referral codes in the links you set up).

SEE ALSO **11.21** "How does eBay's Store Referral Credit program work?"

5.16 "What is a classified ad on eBay?"

EBay allows you to place a classified ad on their site for the purpose of attracting and instructing customers to contact you. You can sell items, services, or properties. You can even include a link to your own website.

The biggest advantage of this feature is that you can get a lot of traffic from eBay instead of having to pay for typical Pay Per Click ads (PPCs) on Google or other search engines. EBay charges a one-time fee for a 30-day ad. In addition, there is no bidding, additional selling fees, or feedback associated with classified ads. It essentially is a lead generator for your product or service for a flat fee.

I think this is the way of the future for eBay sellers with websites. To learn more, select the **Help** link and type **classified ads.**

Setting up Your Seller Preferences

5.17 "How do I set up my eBay seller preferences?"

You can do this very easily in your preferences settings from your My eBay page. Here's how to set up your seller preferences to send automatic invoices and manage payments from your buyers:

1. Go to your My eBay page. Scroll down the left column, and under the My Account section select **Site Preferences.**

2. At this point, you can view all your preference options. You will click on the **Show** link of each preference you wish to change and make the adjustments as you require.

3.   Under the "Payment from Buyers" preference, check the following checkboxes:

❏   Use checkout.

❏   Offer PayPal as a payment method in all my listings.

❏   Display PayPal preferred on my listings.

❏   Tell buyers that I prefer PayPal payments.

❏   Include my items when buyers pay all their sellers at once using PayPal.

❏   Allow buyers to edit payment totals. During checkout, this allows international buyers to adjust the shipping charge to the amount you quoted them. Just double-check that the price they enter is correct. If you are hesitant about this, leave it turned off and send these customers an invoice.

❏   Always use this payment address.

❏   Click **Submit.**

Now continue on to set up your selling preferences, member-to-member communication preferences, and general preferences as you require. The choices here are entirely up to you.

Other Advanced Selling Questions

5.18   "How many days should I give my bidders to respond when I provide a Second Chance Offer?"

I have found that a quick deadline works better than a long one. I either give them three or five days depending on the item. For most items, I recommend that you offer three days.

The best result is also to send the Second Chance Offer immediately after the auction ends (within an hour, if possible). A quick deadline sent immediately to the bidder has three positive marketing results. First, it provides your disappointed (losing) bidder an opportunity to purchase the item at a lower price than the winning bidder paid. Second, it keeps your bidder connected with you before he moves on to another seller's auction. Third, a quick deadline gives a sense of urgency that he needs to act now.

A three-day Second Chance Offer is essentially saying to your bidder, "You lost the item in the bidding process. However, I am offering this item to you at an even better price than the winning bidder paid. Decide quickly before the offer expires." Many will accept it.

SEE ALSO 3.13 "What is a Second Chance Offer?"

5.19 "Should I use audio or video clips in listings?"

This is a relatively new tool that a few eBay sellers are now using. For the most part, I have not been a big fan of the technology. That is, until I recently discovered a company called Deal4it. I am very impressed with their product and the impact it has had on increasing the number of hits, bids, and sales for the sellers who are using it.

Deal4it has developed one of the most inventive ideas I have seen in a long time to improve the eBay buying experience. I also think they have brought the fun back to eBay buying. Using professional actors, they have created numerous interactive video clips that communicate with the buyer and help encourage them to bid.

Here is how it works. Let's say you have a Best Offer listing. As a buyer is viewing your listing, an actor walks into the screen and begins talking. She encourages the buyer to make a bid. If he does, the actor will talk to him again, "No, sorry. That bid is a bit too low" or eventually, "Congratulations, we have accepted your bid!" You can choose from many actors as different characters, in order to portray the mood you want to convey—from serious to very funny.

The results have been excellent. I think buyers enjoy coming back to these listings and also sending their friends there, too: "Hey, check out this funny eBay listing."

It is very simple to add their videos to your listings. Deal4it also offers a very reasonable payment plan whereby you deposit a small amount to start and they will deduct a small fee each time you use their technology in one of your listings. Note the fee is based on one listing, not each time it is used during the listing.

To experience these fun interactive videos, and for a free trial, go to www.deal4it.com/studentrate. Click **View a Demo.**

5.20 "What is the HTML tab for in the Sell Your Item form?"

The Hyper Text Markup Language (HTML) tab enables sellers to easily insert HTML code into their listings. This is usually done to create a different look, format, background, template, and so on. I use the HTML tab to insert tables into my listings for a nice presentation of item specifics. I also use it to easily insert the code from Deal4it mentioned in the previous question.

5.21 "Should I do anything different when accepting payments for an expensive item?"

When selling higher-priced items or automobiles, motorcycles, RVs, and boats, consider using an escrow service. The one eBay recommends is www.escrow.com.

5.22 "Where can I find trade shows for the items I sell?"

You can find almost every major trade show in the United States from the Trade Show News Network at www.tsnn.com. Also, subscribe to magazines, websites, and newsletters that cover the products you sell. This is especially true for hobbyist magazines and websites.

Google the trade show if you know the name, or Google categories of products you are interested in, along with the keywords trade show, exhibit, or conference. For International Asian Trade shows, use http://tradeshow.globalsources.com.

5.23 "Should I charge sales tax? If so, how?"

Sellers who have a profitable eBay business need to collect state sales tax. Simply use the drop-down menu from the Additional Information page during listing creation and choose your state and appropriate local sales tax. Ask your tax advisor or Google your state's Department of Business Licensing if unsure what percentage to charge.

When buyers from outside your state (including international buyers) purchase items from you, no sales tax is shown during checkout. If buyers are from the same state where you live, the tax rate and applicable tax is added to their sale during checkout. PayPal then will collect the tax and place it in your account. You can easily find the tax collected over a certain period by downloading a history report and viewing it using Excel. It is your responsibility, then, to report the collected taxes quarterly or annually. Again, talk to your CPA or tax advisor for questions and further details.

SEE ALSO **13.9** "I don't have Quickbooks. Can I download my PayPal records into an Excel spreadsheet?"

5.24 "My listing was cancelled by eBay. What happened?"

Active listings are sometimes removed from eBay for a variety of reasons. Usually it is because an item violated one of eBay's policies. Potentially fraudulent items, prohibited or restricted items, or keyword spamming are all common reasons for a listing cancellation.

Sometimes another member may have actually reported the item to eBay. Usually, however, the item was flagged by proprietary eBay software that automatically searches for potential listing violations.

If your listing was cancelled and you feel it was unwarranted, you can appeal the decision by following the instructions in the e-mail notification. If it is then ruled a mistake, your eBay fees will be credited to your account and you are free to relist the item.

5.25 "What is Turbo Lister?"

It is a listing tool designed by eBay to replace their Sell Your Item (SYI) form and provide a better, more efficient method of listing creation. It is different from the SYI because it is a database application that you download and then install on your hard drive. All of the listings you then create are on your own hard drive and under your control. This is important because with eBay's SYI, listings are deleted after 90 days. With Turbo Lister, however, you decide when to delete your listings, if ever.

I use Turbo Lister to easily create, duplicate, and edit all my listings. This makes it very quick to create similar listings with the same item but only in a different size or color. Turbo Lister is available free of charge at http://pages.ebay.com/turbo_lister.

5.26 "Which product-analysis tools do you use and recommend?"

I subscribe to three different product-analysis tools. Each serves a different purpose for eBay and Internet research and product sourcing. If I used just one, I would not receive a complete picture of the entire online marketplace. The combination of all three, however, provides accurate, complete information for product-sourcing and listing-creation decisions.

HammerTap

HammerTap removes the product-sourcing guesswork for me. I use it to determine if products I am thinking of selling on eBay will be profitable. I determine this before I even purchase the items for resale.

Worldwide Brands

Most eBay sellers study only eBay statistics. This is a mistake. Serious sellers realize that their competition is not only on eBay but on the Internet. I use Worldwide Brands's Instant Market Research analysis tools to determine the chance of success for items that I am thinking of purchasing for resale.

I simply type the keywords of the product and within seconds I can determine the demand, competition, and overall probability for the product's success. I can also quickly find the suppliers of the product and whether they are wholesalers, importers, liquidators, or drop shippers. In fact, Worldwide Brands is the only drop-ship directory provider certified by eBay.

Instant Market Research tools are included in Worldwide Brands's Product Sourcing Membership. They also have developed an outstanding education program for finding products and working with suppliers called The Whole $ale eBiz Education program. Find out more or receive a membership discount at www.worldwidebrands.com/studentrate.

What Do I Sell®

I use www.whatdoisell.com/studentrate to keep up with the latest product trends on eBay. The site is managed by Lisa Suttora who is considered the product-sourcing guru for eBay sellers. With her insights, I am able to stay ahead of the product curve and sell products that are gaining popularity, demand, and sales momentum.

I also use this site when looking for product suppliers, and especially liquidators. Lisa provides access to her supplier-approved databases for a variety of product categories. If a supplier is in her database, I know they are reputable and I feel confident to order from them.

POWERSELLER TIP

I use Lisa's site along with my research, analysis tools, and methods. Whenever I visit a supplier's website that Lisa has recommended, I scan their site looking for potential products. When I find a product of interest, I pull up HammerTap and Instant Market Research to conduct a quick product search. I will know in seconds whether that product will be profitable on eBay. I show you step-by-step how I do this on my website. Go to www.trainingu4auctions.com and click the **Research a Product** link.

5.27 "What is the eBay Toolbar?"

The eBay Toolbar is a free, downloadable tool. When installed, it will reside on your web browser. You can use it to quickly search for items on eBay or the web at any time.

One of the best features is the Account Guard. This provides an indicator that turns "green" whenever you are on a genuine eBay or PayPal site. You can also enter your eBay and PayPal passwords into the toolbar. Then if you accidently enter the same password into a non-eBay/PayPal site, the toolbar will give you a warning.

This is an excellent tool to foil spoof e-mail crooks that send you to phony eBay or PayPal sites. Download the eBay Toolbar for your web browser at http://pages.ebay.com/ebay_toolbar.

6 International Selling

Selling internationally on eBay is certainly rewarding. The e-mails that I receive first thing in the morning are usually from my international buyers many miles and time zones away.

One morning I opened my e-mails and noticed there were several orders, some with questions from buyers that I promptly answered. As I was pouring my second cup of coffee, I realized that in only 20 minutes I had just communicated with my customers in Austria, France, the UK, Greece, Australia, and Hong Kong. What a fun business, indeed!

Avoiding International Fraud

6.1 **"I am hesitant to sell items internationally, but I know I can increase my sales by doing so. Should I be concerned?"**

Depending on the season and the items that I list, about 15–30 percent of my sales are international. In fact, some of my best and friendliest customers live in France, Greece, Italy, the UK, and Australia.

Remember that international bidders who partake in bidding on your item drive the price higher. Therefore, even if international buyers are not the winning bidder, you will receive a higher final price on your item because of their bids.

However, I do not recommend that sellers who are new to eBay sell internationally. The reason is that new sellers tend to make beginner mistakes. I would prefer that these lessons are learned when dealing with the customer from Michigan, not Greece.

Be careful when listing heavy or oversized items for sale globally. The cost to ship them can be very expensive. I also do not recommend that you sell inexpensive items (less than $20) globally. It is not time-effective or cost-effective to sell and ship these items to another country.

POWERSELLER TIP

After you have the experience of making several sales and begin selling more valuable products that have a global appeal, I encourage you to sell internationally. However, you need to do so wisely. Read this entire chapter as well as Chapter 10 on international shipping before you proceed. This amount of information will help you make wise choices as to the expanse of your sales. Where and when you sell is strictly your decision, based on your experience and comfort zone.

6.2 "Are there certain countries that I should not ship to?"

Yes, certain countries are known for fraud. EBay has reported that those countries are Nigeria, Indonesia, and Romania. You can check for the latest scams against eBay sellers at www.millersmiles.co.uk/search/eBay. See the next question.

6.3 "How can I stop buyers from bidding on my items if they live in a country where I do not want to ship?"

Sellers who ship internationally can set up their preferences to block bidders who live in a country where they do not want to ship. This is a two-step process:

First, set your Buyer Requirement Preferences as follows:

1. Login to your eBay account.

2. Go to your My eBay, and under the **My Account** tab select **Site Preferences.**

3. Under Selling Preferences select **Show** under **Buyer Requirements.**

4. Select **Edit** under **Block buyers who.**

5. Place a check mark next to **Block buyers who are registered in countries to which I don't ship.**

6. Click **Submit.**

Second, when you are creating your listings, and come to the "Ship to" portion, select **Will ship to the United States** and then choose all other countries where you will ship. EBay will then block buyers who live outside your accepted country list from bidding on your item.

Communication and Payment

6.4 "How can I communicate with my international customers? Does eBay perform some type of language translation?"

EBay does not translate languages in either listings or e-mails. If international buyers are shopping on the United States eBay site (www.ebay.com) or viewing your listing on an international eBay site, then they most likely can read and write some English. When you receive their e-mails, you will notice distinct expressions in their writing based on their native language. It is actually a lot of fun reading these e-mails.

When I communicate with my customers, I tend to use the same terms they use. For example, buyers from the United Kingdom may use the words "regards" when they sign off. They do not customarily use "thank you" or "sincerely."

French, Italian, Greek, and some German buyers will usually call me friend such as "Hello, friend" or "Thank you, friend." I address and close e-mails to them in the same way. Many Australians will start their e-mails with "G'day" and may end with "Watch out for the crocs!" I sometimes respond with "Greetings from Seattle!"

My best tip for sending e-mails to non-English-speaking countries is to keep your e-mails very brief. Again, some of these customers probably only understand a limited amount of English. Speaking from experience, if you ramble on with a five-paragraph answer, you may quite likely get a return e-mail like this one that I received:

Ciao, friend,

Sorry, my English, but understand is difficult. Again with logic explain, please?

Thank you, friend,
Vincenzio

Keep your response e-mails to non-English-speaking countries to one or two sentences and get right to the point. That seems to work.

If you are having a hard time communicating, you can try to translate your e-mails to another language by going to Google, clicking on the **Language Tools** link, and using the translate-text tool. I have done this when I have received feedback in French or Italian. You can find another popular and free language translation tool at www. freetranslation.com. Just keep in mind that software translation is never as good as using someone who speaks the language. Nevertheless, it can give you an idea of whether their feedback was good or bad, or the nature of their question.

6.5 "How do I receive payments from international customers?"

With PayPal. In fact, receiving international payments is much the same as receiving domestic payments. PayPal is now available in over 190 countries and regions and most likely is in the country where your buyer lives. Just state plainly in your policies that you accept PayPal payments from international customers.

International buyers will receive an invoice from eBay (in their native language) with the equivalent currency requested in U.S. dollars. They will most likely pay you in U.S. dollars. If they pay with Euros or another currency, it will be in the equivalent U.S. dollar amount. You will be notified of the payment with an e-mail from PayPal, and you can choose to accept the currency or insist on U.S. dollars only.

6.6 "Is it okay to ship an item to an international buyer with an unconfirmed address?"

Probably. At the time of this writing, only PayPal customers in the United States, Canada, and the UK can be confirmed. Check the buyer's feedback from other eBay sellers. If it looks satisfactory, then it should be okay to ship to this customer. Your PayPal seller protection is now available to all countries where PayPal is accepted.

SEE ALSO   **1.31 "What is a Confirmed address?"**

SEE ALSO   **1.34 "What is PayPal's Seller Protection Program?"**

6.7 "Is it okay to accept payments from an international buyer who wants to use Western Union, MoneyGram, or a personal check?"

No. These payment methods are a frequent source of fraud and you want no part of it. These requests are actually less common now than even a couple of years ago. Most international buyers are now using PayPal. Through e-mail exchanges, I have even helped international buyers sign up for a PayPal account.

Electronic payments are now the only form accepted by eBay. PayPal should be available in the country where your customer lives.

6.8 "How can I avoid fraudulent payments from international buyers?"

You can avoid the vast majority of trouble from dishonest international buyers if you strictly follow three rules. Make sure that rules one and two are in the payment policy of your listings.

Rule #1: EBay now only accepts online payments from your domestic and international customers. Never agree to go outside of this payment method.

Rule #2: Never ship the item until you have been paid and PayPal has cleared the funds.

Rule #3: Set up your Buyer requirements properly to block bidders from countries known for fraud.

SEE ALSO 6.3 "How can I stop buyers from bidding on items if they live in a country where I do not want to ship?"

Other International Selling Questions

6.9 "Who is responsible if I sell and ship an item to a country where that item is prohibited?"

It is the responsibility of the seller not to sell or ship any item to a country where it is prohibited. Remember also that just because an item is allowed in the United States does not mean it is permitted in other countries. These items typically include alcohol, tobacco, firearms and other weapons, pharmaceuticals, narcotics, certain foods, and other items that are prohibited or quota-restricted in that particular country.

If you sell any item that may be prohibited, it is best to check the import restrictions for the countries where you want to sell. Go to http://pe.usps.gov/text/imm/immctry.htm and click on the countries where you wish to sell.

You can also conduct an Internet search for a particular country's Customs website. If the restrictions are not obvious from their site, contact them through e-mail and ask for a list of restricted or prohibited items. Two fairly good websites to learn the basics of exporting restrictions are www.export.gov/exportbasics and www.wcoomd.org.

6.10 "Where can I find additional information about selling internationally?"

On eBay, refer to http://pages.ebay.com/globaltrade. Other helpful sites are the following:

- www.export.gov
- www.wcoomd.org
- www.export.gov/exportbasics
- www.sba.gov/aboutsba/sbaprograms/internationaltrade

I also provide significant detail about international selling and shipping in my book, *eBay Business at Your Fingertips.*

6.11 "What is the International Site Visibility listing upgrade?"

When creating your listings, this upgrade is how you choose to have your item appear on international eBay sites. The listing will appear the same on these sites as they do on eBay.com.

You need to meet certain seller requirements, such as a Feedback Rating of 10 and a Verified PayPal account. Remember when creating these listings that you will need to determine your international shipping rates and policies. To learn more, select the **Help** link and type **international site visibility**.

7 General eBay Questions

There are eBay questions, problems, and solutions that can't necessarily be categorized. However, they are equally important, and for that reason they have been grouped·in this chapter.

7.1 "I just received a negative feedback. What should I do?"

First, don't panic. Although it is certainly disappointing, if you have several other positive feedbacks, it will hardly have any effect on your sales. After several more sales and a few pages of positive comments, the negative feedback comment becomes buried and almost no one will dig that deep to read it.

You can respond to the negative feedback by selecting the **Reply to Feedback** link on your Feedback page in My eBay. Remember that the way you respond to the feedback may mean more to the next buyer than the fact that you received a negative mark. If you goofed, admit it and state what your resolution was. That turns a negative into a positive.

If the feedback was unwarranted, you can appeal to the buyer and try to work it out. If she agrees, then you can formally request that she either change or remove the negative feedback.

Remember also that negative and neutral feedback will be removed from your feedback percentage after one year. For more information, select **Help,** then type **negative feedback.**

7.2 "I want to sell a certain item that is sometimes known for fakes. How can I be sure if the item I am selling is genuine?"

This is a very good question, but nearly impossible to answer. If it is an expensive item, you may need to conduct considerable research and try to obtain a certificate of authenticity for the item.

As the seller, the responsibility for not selling a fake is yours. Where did you get the item? Did the seller provide a certificate of authenticity? What guarantees did he make that it was a genuine product? Does the seller specialize in these items or was this a one-time sale? Is the seller a professional dealer or do you suspect he's an amateur? If an amateur, the seller may not have any more of an idea whether the item is genuine than you do. He may even be selling fakes unintentionally and never realize it. You need to conduct further research to guarantee authenticity.

Because you are the seller, your feedback rating is at risk, so you need to verify authenticity. Is this a one-time sale or are you going to sell many of these items in your product line? If these will be part of your product line, then you need to become an expert yourself and know how to spot a fake.

You can start by contacting other professional sellers of the item and ask them questions about authenticity (many of the top sellers of items prone to fakes have written "eBay Guides" about how to spot fakes of that item). You may even find an expert. If so, ask them how to spot not only a fake item, but also a fake certificate. Ask them what websites, blogs, books, and periodicals they recommend on the subject. Search the Internet for the item's name along with keywords such as "fake, replica, knock-off, copy, counterfeit, phony, fraud."

If you will be selling many of these items or if it is expensive, then consider acquiring a certificate of authenticity. There are a few authenticity services available. They charge a fee based on the detail and time required. You will most likely need to send a photo or several photos of your item to them. You can find authenticity services that are eBay-approved by going to the **Help** link and typing **authentication** in the search box field.

POWERSELLER TIP

If you plan to sell items that are known for knock-offs, eventually someone will report you to eBay or give negative feedback claiming you sold them a fake—even when it was genuine. Is this really the type of product that you want to sell on eBay? I like to avoid trouble, not jump into the middle of it.

7.3 "What do you do with your eBay business when you go on vacation?"

I travel quite a bit on business, so a lot depends on how long I will be away. If it is just for a few days or a weekend, I don't change anything. I take my laptop with me to check e-mails and answer any questions a buyer may have. Any sales that occur while I am away can easily be filled as soon as I return. Because I ship most items by Priority Mail, the customer will still receive the item quickly and will never even know I was not at my office when he placed his order.

If I am away for several days on business, my wife fills the orders. For true vacations, however, I have a few other options, all of which I have used on occasion.

Do you have a partner or an eBay seller friend who can fill your orders while you are away? If so, great; that is your answer. You can return the favor for her when she is away on vacation.

When I don't have anyone who can fill in for me, I make sure that all my auctions end at least one week before I leave for vacation. That way, the payments will arrive and I can fill the orders within that week.

Before I leave, I upload all my auction listings to eBay and schedule them to "kick off" while I am away. I just make sure they are all true auctions and that there are no Fixed Price listings. That way, all the buyers can be bidding on my items while I am having fun in the sun. I take my laptop with me and check any questions once a day. I schedule the items to end the day I return. So the day after I return, I do the entire order fulfillment.

If you also have an eBay Store, eBay makes it easy to temporarily close your store. You simply go to your store, click the **Seller Manage Store** link at the bottom of the page, then under the **Related Links** section at the bottom left, select **Store Vacation Settings.**

You now have a few choices. You can place a large banner on your store that everyone will see, such as "We are attending a trade show. Feel free to shop and purchase any item. We will ship your item upon our return on (enter your date)."

You can also just place a banner that your store is temporarily closed and choose to let eBay hide all your store items from view. If someone visits your store, she will see only your banner but no items. As soon as you return, you allow the items to be viewed again and they all appear instantly. This is a great feature that enables you to easily close the store without having to take your listings down and then having to relist them again when you return.

7.4 "What is a Dutch Auction?"

A Dutch Auction, now called a Multiple Item Auction, is one where a seller lists two or more of the same item using an Auction-Style format. There can be multiple winners in a Dutch Auction. Therefore the purpose of bidding on the auction is to determine how the quantity of the items will be divided between the winning bidders.

The highest bidders get their quantities filled first. The next highest bidder then has her quantity filled, then the next highest bidder, and so on until the quantity is depleted. However, after the auction closes, they will all pay the same price as the *lowest* winning bid.

If you are confused, think of it this way: As a buyer, you want to bid high enough to be sure you get the quantity you want. From the seller's view, however, you had better be sure that the starting bid is the minimum amount you want for the items. If the number of bidders is low, and the winning bid is only for the starting bid amount, the entire quantity could sell for the starting bid price.

The lesson learned is not to list multiple quantities in an Auction-Style listing unless you are willing to let everything go for the starting bid. In other words, set your starting bid at the lowest price you are willing to accept for everything. If this is all still confusing, learn more by selecting the **Help** link on eBay and typing **Dutch Auction** in the search box.

Personally, I rarely recommend using a Dutch Auction unless you just want to get rid of several items and profit is not your main goal. Instead, I recommend using other ways to move multiple quantities:

- Create a multiple-item Fixed Price listing.
- List one item at auction and then send Second Chance Offers after the auction ends to every bidder whose bid amount is acceptable to you.

SEE ALSO   3.13 "What is a Second Chance Offer?"

SEE ALSO   5.18 "How many days should I give my bidders to respond
when I provide a Second Chance Offer?"

7.5 "What is My eBay?"

A link to your My eBay page can be found at the very top of every
page on eBay. Every important event that is happening now or has
recently happened between you and eBay is tracked here. This is a
welcome convenience, as you won't have to keep your own records of
events and transactions. Following are a few examples of the important links at your fingertips in your My eBay page:

- Account Information
- Buying Activities
- Selling Activities
- Messages

7.6 "What is the difference between an About Me page
and a My World page?"

An About Me or My World page should be used to provide other eBay
members or potential customers with important information about
you or your eBay business. Every eBay member can have both an
About Me page and a My World page. A My World page is automatically provided whether you decide to customize it or not. An About
Me page requires that you create the page. There is no charge to have
either or both pages.

A My World page is more structured. Members must choose templates
from preformatted sections. It has a bio section available where you
talk about yourself, and a guest book section where guests can sign
their name or leave comments. It is also more restrictive because you
can display only one picture compared to an About Me page where
you can have as many pictures as you want. You can find a member's
My World page by clicking on his **User ID** link.

An About Me page allows for more customization. You can add several
pictures and use HTML coding to give your page a more distinctive

look. You can even add a link to your website. When you create an About Me page, a "me" logo appears next to your User ID. It will also be the same page used for your **About the Seller** link if you own an eBay Store.

7.7 "I am an artist, photographer, musician, or writer, and I want to sell my work on eBay. What are my chances for success?"

They don't call unknown artists "starving" for nothing. Unfortunately, unless you are already a well-known artist, your chances for making any money selling your form of art on eBay are very slim.

If I wanted to quickly decorate a new home or office building with artwork, I would shop on eBay. I can sometimes buy art prints for as low as $1. So while it is a great place to shop, don't expect to make any money here.

You would probably do much better renting a booth at a local trade show or fair. You could also open an eBay Store and use it as your website, or create your own website. This way, potential customers you meet at trade shows can purchase from you later.

I recommend you use more traditional methods of selling your form of talent and try to build a local following. Make as many connections in your art as possible and then network your way to stardom.

7.8 "My sales are waning. Is eBay too saturated now to make any money?"

The eBay marketplace is fluid and it moves at a rapid pace. Fads and trends come and go. What was hot or fashionable even six months ago may not be hot now. Maybe new, tough competition has moved into your categories.

In most cases, when sellers ask me this question I ask them, "Have you become stagnant by continuing to sell the same items over and over again without expanding your business or moving into new areas, categories, or products?" If yes, then what happened is that the market shifted on you while you stayed put. The eBay marketplace moved on to new, exciting products, and your products became saturated, stale, or less in demand.

The problem is not eBay. The problem is that you did not shift with the eBay marketplace to new products with high demand. See the next two questions.

7.9 "I am selling a lot of products but at the end of the month, it seems that I am not making that much money. What am I doing wrong?"

This happened to me when I first started selling as well. So the advice below is what I did when I finally realized (and had to admit) what my problem was. Namely, the problem was me.

There are now well over 1 million people who make a part-time income or full-time living selling on eBay. That is an important fact to keep in mind. Profitable eBay businesses can be and are being run.

Remember that the sole responsibility for the profitability of your business resides not with eBay, but with you. EBay is merely the sales channel that brings the customers to your business. So don't blame eBay if you are not making the money you desire. Let's look at what you are doing wrong or what you are not doing at all. There could be several reasons for this situation.

- You have not yet truly found profitable products or niches and therefore continue to sell the wrong products.
- You haven't expanded your product line.
- The competition has increased.
- Market demand for your products has shifted and most likely diminished.

Although it could be a combination of any or all of these, my experienced hunch is that the main problem is the first bullet. Take a simple test for your business. Write down all the items you sell, the profit you make on each item (remember to subtract all the eBay and Pay-Pal fees), and the average number of those items sold per month. Get a calculator and seriously do the math.

Now add up all your net profit and compare that to what you desire for your monthly profit. If it's not adding up to what you want to make, your problem is simple and obvious: you are not selling enough profitable items. It is as simple as that.

If you thought that was a real "Well, duh," so did I when it first occurred to me. Here is another gem—who is in charge of choosing the products that you are selling? *You!*

Consider this realization your eBay wake-up call. Now here is the good news: because you are causing the problem, you can fix it!

Look more closely at your products:

- Are you selling the same products that you were six months or a year ago, or maybe even three years ago?
- Are those products still profitable? Were they ever profitable?
- Did your competition change?
- Did you even study your competition or did you remain myopic?
- Did the demand change for your products?
- Has your supplier changed and/or are you now paying more for your products?
- Have you added any new profitable products in the last few months?
- Did you get lethargic and stop looking for new products?
- Do you make product decisions using supply, demand, and competitive analysis or are those decisions based on hunches and whims?
- Do you conduct your eBay research first to ensure that the items you want to sell will be profitable—and only then do you purchase your merchandise?

Please be honest with yourself for a minute. Have you actually been applying these critically important business success factors?

Have you done your research, found your niche, developed a solid business plan and product line, or are you just selling items that you picked up simply because they were cheap, easily available, or items you stumbled across and bought on a whim? Have you been following a definite marketing plan or has your product selection been trial and error with hit-or-miss results?

My guess is that you are getting out of your business exactly what you are putting into it (speaking from experience). Remember, you are running a business, not a hobby. The eBay marketplace is fluid. What was hot a year ago may not be moving this year. You must stay on top of these trends and changes, and move with the marketplace (see WhatDoISell® in 4.67).

When this happened to me, I had to move out of my comfort zone and get serious about my business. Maybe I wanted to sell colorful plastic cowboy hat covers (a fictional example). However, after a few months of disappointing sales, yes, I had to admit that I was selling the wrong products. Maybe I would make more money selling spark plugs and auto accessories. However, I had not even bothered to research that area because I kept trying to sell all those plastic cowboy hat covers I had picked up at a liquidation sale simply because they were cheap.

I was selling the wrong products on eBay and I had to admit it. So I decided, "Don't force it; face it."

Does this sound like you as well? *Rich Dad, Poor Dad* author Robert T. Kiyosaki wrote that his rich dad told him, "Losers quit when they fail. Winners fail until they succeed." Don't be discouraged. Realizing your problem is the first step toward success. So you got it wrong. Learn from your mistakes, take off your blinders, and move on to profitable products in profitable categories and niches.

Put your eBay business on autopilot for a few days and start looking at other niches and categories. Use HammerTap and Worldwide Brands's Instant Market Research to help streamline your product research and analysis. Move on from the products you are selling and become a profitable business. Keep looking for new items and stay on top of eBay trends and market demands. It is your business, so it is your job.

What I have just described is the true secret to eBay success that seems so elusive to many sellers. Step away, make a new plan, and move forward. In fact, I provide a complete method for exactly how to find profitable products and avoid the losers in the companion to this book, *eBay Rescue Profit Maker.*

SEE ALSO   5.26 "Which product-analysis tools do you use and recommend?"

SEE ALSO **4.67** "How can I stay current with everything that is happening on eBay?"

7.10 "Do you think I should leave my job and make eBay my full-time business?"

Don't quit your day job … at least not yet. Developing a solid eBay business that can actually replace your salary will take a lot of time and money (for product inventory). If you don't have the luxury of seed money for your company, plus additional, sufficient funds to pay yourself a salary for several months while you are building your business, then keep your job and make eBay selling your part-time business.

There are many commercials on the radio or infomercials on TV that promise quick wealth with eBay or the Internet. They usually have prepackaged books, tapes, CDs, and DVDs that will be your complete guide to building an eBay or Internet business. Many will claim that you can buy all your products from their "warehouse," so you don't even have to look for items to sell. Beware when you see these claims. They are most likely middlemen or outright scams.

SEE ALSO **12.22** "What are middlemen?"

Maybe some individual did indeed hit the mother lode on eBay and his story is covered in a periodical or newspaper. The problem is, this leaves an impression that it's easy to make a lot of money on eBay, quickly.

While it is true that some of the prepackaged courses mentioned in infomercials can contain very useful information, you cannot buy a prepackaged, cookie-cutter eBay business and expect it to be successful. The reason is obvious. If it is cookie cutter, then everyone who purchases that program is doing the same thing, buying their items from the same source, and selling the same items on eBay. Those sellers have unbelievably high competition.

Many give it a try, get discouraged, or get smart and quit. Who do they bad mouth? Is it the source of their bad information? No, they blame eBay!

An eBay business is just like any other entrepreneurial start-up business. You don't discover the mother lode in a week and have success instantly fall into your lap. You have to develop your business. There will be a lot of upfront work discovering your niche and then constant searching, testing, and weeding out products. You will also be listing items, packing and shipping items, and discovering and working with new distributors and new products. This is the never-ending cycle of an eBay business.

There is a saying that entrepreneurs work 14 hours a day for themselves so they don't have to work 8 hours a day for someone else. To be successful on eBay, you will quite likely be working harder than you do at the job you now have.

While this has proven true for me, I would also add, "AND LOVING IT!" This has been more enjoyable and rewarding work than any position I held during my 23-year corporate career. I sincerely wish the same satisfaction and rewarding eBay career for you.

Forget the hype, and especially stay away from the infomercial "quacks." Following standard business practices, along with hard work and persistence, is your best chance to develop your own gold vein eBay mother lode. See the next two questions.

7.11 "What are the reasons that eBay sellers fail?"

There are, of course, many reasons for an eBay business to fail. Usually, however, it is one or more of the following reasons:

- The business was undercapitalized.
- Frustration with or no help, support, or encouragement from spouse or family.
- Costly mistakes such as buying large amounts of merchandise to sell on eBay that is not profitable.
- No business plan. Product and business decisions are based on hunches.
- Treating the business as a hobby.
- Not paying attention to financial or sales metrics.
- Little effort put forth. Getting lazy or careless.

7.12 "What are the key components for a successful eBay business?"

The short answer is the opposite of everything listed in the previous question:

- Ensure that you have enough financial capital to purchase your products and supplies during lean times.

- Ask for help from family members. Assign tasks such as who answers the e-mails, orders the products, takes the pictures, creates the listings, packs the items, and goes to the post office.

- Conduct eBay research to determine that the products you sell will be profitable before you purchase them.

- Develop a business plan and work the plan. What will you sell, where will you get your products, how will you market your business? Determine what you consider success.

- Treat it like a business, not a hobby. Think like a retailer.

- Learn how to take professional-looking pictures.

- Learn how to create enticing listings that draw the most hits and beat your competition.

- Sell only profitable items. Constantly weed out and replenish your product line.

- Stay on top of trends. Join local eBay support groups and subscribe to newsletters.

- One word—perseverance!

Photography

The photos you use are just as important as any other factor for creating a successful eBay listing. They can provide a favorable first impression. After a buyer completes a keyword search, she will scan the listings looking at price, shipping, and the gallery picture. If the item's price and shipping rate are about the same between sellers, the gallery picture you display can be the deciding factor whether she will click on your listing or your competitor's.

Photography Equipment

8.1 "What camera do you recommend for eBay photography?"

I don't recommend a particular brand or model. Almost every digital camera sold today will meet your needs for eBay pictures. However, in my opinion, there are a few features your camera should have for taking eBay pictures:

- Must have a Macro mode (the ability to take close-up pictures).
- Option to turn off the flash.
- Ability to white balance.
- An easy way to download the pictures to your computer.
- An ample-sized LCD display on the back of the camera so you can clearly see what you're taking.
- A battery that comes with a long charge or the option to plug the camera into a power source. If you are taking several pictures, it may drain your batteries and the camera will keep shutting off during your photography session.
- Ability to mount the camera on a tripod or camera stand.

- A video-out jack so you can hook your camera directly to a portable TV or computer located next to your photography setup. Now you can get a much better view of your shot rather than only using the camera's LCD screen.

You should be able to find a camera with all of these features for about $150–$300. There is a lot of good camera comparison information at www.cnet.com. A great place to look for deals on cameras is eBay.

8.2 "What do you recommend for a photography backdrop?"

You can't get any simpler than an ironed white sheet. You can also use white butcher paper or poster board. These backgrounds will work for a temporary setup, especially if you are only trying to sell a few household items.

For a better display, a colored background can enhance the look of your item and make it stand out from your competition. Photography stores sell rolls of different-colored backgrounds. You can even use rolls of wallpaper, as long as the background is plain or subtle. Also visit a fabric store and purchase a few different colors of fabric for your photography backgrounds. To start with, I suggest each of these colors: white, gray, and royal blue. If you desire a velvet background (which is nice for jewelry), I suggest black, navy, or red velvet.

When deciding which background to use, you need a good contrasting color to make the item stand out from the background. Hold the object up to each color. Whichever one makes the object jump out at you like 3D, that is your pick. Taking a few extra moments to consider and then select the best background is one more way your overall listing and presentation will look professional.

8.3 "What do you recommend for photography lighting?"

If you need professional-quality lighting, visit a photography store or search photography websites such as www.dpreview.com. If you need standard lighting, go to a discount or home-improvement store and purchase two inexpensive gooseneck lamps with a minimum 60-watt rating (higher is even better). The lamps can be tabletop or floor-standing. I prefer the tabletops, as they are easier to maneuver and can be placed closer to an object. I don't recommend the ones with clamps, as you can't always clamp the lamp where you want it.

To eliminate the yellow glow from incandescent lights, use fluorescent daylight bulbs. Fluorescent bulbs are also best because of low heat. Fluorescent bulbs also require less wattage and last a very long time. The ones I use are "daylight" fluorescent bulbs (the ones that look like a corkscrew) that are "balanced" (meaning the light spectrum emitted is equivalent to natural light at noon). Get the highest wattage bulbs you can find that do not exceed the rating for your lamps.

8.4 "What are diffusers?"

You will need to diffuse the light to keep from having those bright bulb "hot spot" reflections on your item. Photography stores and photography websites have diffusers available for purchase. If you want to do this cheaply, white tissue paper (vellum), an opaque shower curtain, or even a white sheet will work as a diffuser. Certain light-colored opaque cloths will also diffuse light. Check for these types of cloth when you are picking out your backgrounds at fabric stores.

Keep in mind that these ordinary materials such as tissue paper, shower curtains, or cloth will stand up to any heat from fluorescent bulbs. Just keep them away from those very hot bulbs—especially halogen. You sure don't want your local fire department interrupting your photography session!

8.5 "What are reflectors?"

You should use reflectors to refocus the light to remove shadows from your shot. I use thin, white pieces of Styrofoam, available from craft stores, that are sturdy enough to stand up on their own, and then cut them to the size I need (usually about 8" high by 10" long). Once I have my item to be photographed in place and all the side light-ing turned on, I move the reflectors around to capture the light and reflect it to the areas that need fill-lighting. This removes dark areas on the object or shadows behind the item.

8.6 "What do you recommend for an affordable yet professional photography setup?"

When I first started selling on eBay, I bought a tri-fold poster board used for school projects and displays. I attached my background fabrics to the top with binder clips. This was adequate until I started selling smaller and more valuable items and I realized I needed to set myself apart from my competition with more professional-looking photos.

I have searched the marketplace for what I believe are the best photography kits for eBay sellers. These professional kits do a much better job than homemade setups and yet are still very affordable. The additional money you make by taking professional pictures for your auctions will quickly pay for the equipment.

Here are the photography kits I recommend for eBay sellers:

- **Cubes, Tents, and Cocoons:** Photographers use these tools to photograph small- to medium-size items. The material is made to act as a light diffuser. You simply place the item inside the cube, shine the lights through the sides, and place your camera in front of the cube to take the shots you need. You can also place a different-colored background fabric inside the cube.

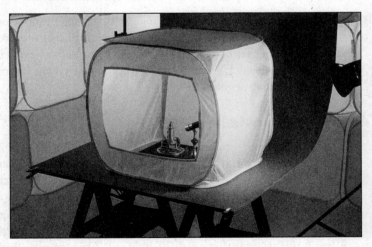

Cloud Cube

- **Cloud Dome:** This product, developed for the forensic industry, is perfect for eBay sellers of jewelry, coins, baseball cards, and any small item that lies flat. You place your background fabric on a table, set the item to be photographed on the fabric, and put the dome over the item. The lights are positioned on the sides, and all light is diffused through the dome. The camera mounts on top of the dome so the shots are taken straight down. The results are remarkable.

Cloud Dome

Photography Tips

8.7 "Do you have any tips for taking eBay pictures?"

Study magazines that have advertisements for the type of items you are selling. Study how professional photographers take pictures of these items. In particular, notice the backgrounds, how the items are arranged, camera angles, lighting, and any props or special effects used.

Choose the best background color for your item. Arrange the item in an attractive way based on examples you have seen in magazines. To help keep items upright, use a small beanbag under the background cloth or a pink pearl eraser behind the object. For larger items, use a can of soup or a liter-size soft-drink container. You can also use Wacky Tacky or Museum putty.

SEE ALSO **8.2 "What do you recommend for a photography backdrop?"**

Check the side lighting and camera angle. Now examine your lighting again while looking at your camera's LCD screen and remove any hot spots or shadows with diffusers and reflectors. Don't agonize over this; just give it some thought for a moment and make the necessary adjustments.

Before you actually take the picture, place a white sheet of paper in front of the item to set your camera's "white balance." This will produce the true color of your item. Now hold your breath and take the shot.

SEE ALSO **8.19 "What does white balance mean?"**

After you download the picture to your computer, using the photo-editing software that came with your camera, crop it tight so there is just a bit of background showing to frame it. Adjust the brightness, contrast, or sharpness if needed (this is rare).

I think the best tip I can give you for eBay photography is to remember that pictures are just as important for your item's success as any other component of your listing. Get the best photography equipment you can afford. Study magazines to learn how professionals take photos of items similar to what you sell. Experiment with your camera and learn how to take great photos. Consider enrolling in a digital photography class at your local community college or community center.

8.8 "How do I photograph artwork that is behind glass that has a glare?"

Shoot it straight on or straight down. Make sure you use diffused or reflected lighting to cut down on the glare. While looking through the LCD viewer, adjust the position and angle of your lights and reflectors to minimize the glare.

If you will be photographing several pieces of art under glass, consider getting a black poster board. Cut a hole in the poster board just large enough for your camera lens. Then attach the poster board to your tripod so only the lens juts through the hole. This cuts down on light that is reflected off the glass and directly back to the camera.

If you want a better solution, consider purchasing a polarizing filter. This is usually used in the larger (SLR) cameras rather than the smaller, portable point-and-shoot cameras. However, you can always just hold the filter in front of the lens when taking the shot.

If you can't remove all of the glare, it's probably acceptable for eBay photography. Just adjust your lights so the reflections are not interfering with the subject of the art.

8.9 "How should I photograph clothing?"

Iron or steam the clothing first. Then neatly lay the clothing on a table with a white background. Shoot the clothing straight down. Another alternative is to pin the clothing (arms out, then folded back in at elbow) with straight pins to a sturdy Styrofoam board, then raise and adjust the board to the proper angle for the camera. Crop the picture very tight so very little background is showing. You can also use a mannequin. See the next question.

8.10 "Should I use a model for clothing?"

I don't recommend models. You want the buyer's full attention on the item, and models can be distracting. Instead, use mannequins. The torso mannequins with no heads are best. You can find them on eBay for a good price. If you do use a model, maybe just crop off the head when editing the picture in your computer.

8.11 "How can I eliminate a moiré pattern in a colorful shirt?"

A moiré pattern on clothing is sometimes produced by conflicting color or fabric patterns. It is more prevalent when the fabric or color lines intersect or are curved rather than running parallel. You sometimes see this on TV when a person is wearing a particular checked or hounds-tooth patterned shirt or jacket. As they move around, the fabric almost looks alive or as if it pulsates.

Digital cameras and especially scanners will sometimes create this annoying pattern. Try rotating the item 90 or 180 degrees so the camera will capture the pattern at a different angle. You can always rotate the picture back in your photo-editing software. Increasing the resolution, especially on a scanner, can also help reduce moiré.

I have also found that a slightly different camera angle, or setting the camera farther away from the object (then zooming in), will help to reduce the undesired effect. If you have photo-editing software, try adjusting the sharpness button. You may never completely remove moiré from a busy-patterned shirt or jacket, but you should be able to reduce the problem.

8.12 "How should I photograph clear glassware?"

Make sure the glass is completely clean and free of fingerprints and smudges. Use as much natural light as possible, even if this means moving your setup close to a window. Remember though that you do not want direct sunlight, but shaded light. Diffuse any side lighting and turn off the camera's flash to avoid as much glare as possible.

For crystal or clear glass, a colored background or plain white or black is suitable. If the glass is colored, use only a white background. The glass should not be on its side, but upright, like it would look if placed on a table.

Take a few pictures from slightly different angles. Then examine the pictures closely when you download them into your photo-editing software. Glassware can be touched up a bit with brightness, contrast, and sharpness (in that order).

8.13 "How should I photograph small jewelry?"

Use the macro setting on your camera and get as close as possible with the item still in focus. Check to see if your camera has a manual or "spot focus" feature.

I like to use the Cloud Dome for jewelry. Otherwise, use diffusers to eliminate the glare when lighting shiny items. Place the camera on a tripod and turn off the flash.

SEE ALSO 8.6 "What do you recommend for an affordable yet professional photography setup?"

If you will be selling a lot of jewelry, then consider purchasing an LED light specifically used to create "sparkles" in gemstones and diamonds. This light is placed in front of the stone to add that sparkle you see in professional photography.

Study jewelry advertisements and department store catalogs to learn how professional photographers place necklaces, watches, bracelets, and other jewelry. Necklaces are nicely displayed on a black velvet (neck only) mannequin. It is best to stand a ring up. I use museum putty (found at craft or photography stores) for this purpose.

POWERSELLER TIP

When creating your listings for jewelry, be sure to choose the Picture Pack option. This enables the buyer to supersize the picture.

8.14 "How should I photograph a large item?"

Place the large item against a neutral-colored wall. Isolate the item from all other clutter in the room. Turn on all the lights in the room and white balance the camera just before you take the shot. Crop the shot tight to minimize the walls and floor.

SEE ALSO 8.19 "What does white balance mean?"

For large items that are maneuverable, use large rolls of white paper to create a background. You can also use large-size white poster boards. With masking tape, lightly attach the paper or poster boards to the wall, down to the floor and then out onto the floor. You now have a usable white background constructed to the size you need. Now place the large item on the white background and crop the shot tight so only a bit of the background shows.

If you have large items in the garage, go ahead and take the pictures in the garage using the white poster board or paper rolls to fashion a background. Open the garage door and place the item in the shade inside the garage. This will provide natural but diffused light. Remember to white balance the camera after everything is set up and all the lights are on.

Other Photography Questions

8.15   **"How should I download and file my pictures so I can easily find them when I am ready to list the item?"**

Every camera is different. Some cameras require a USB cable, some a memory card, and others a base that the camera plugs into to download the pictures. Almost every camera manufacturer provides editing software that comes with the camera. Therefore, the simple answer is, refer to the owner's manual. If you have misplaced your instructions, go to the manufacturer's website and download a new copy.

Once your pictures are downloaded to your computer, you need to name them so they are easy to find later. Don't name them with a number. I suggest you use a date and keyword title. For example, if your item is a red candle, and you are going to list it on 11/23/10, save the picture to a file named "red candle 11.23.10." That is much easier to find later when it is time to upload it to eBay. If the date of the picture is irrelevant, then label it clearly using a descriptive file folder name and filename.

8.16   **"What size and format should my pictures be?"**

The standard size is 400 pixels (on the longest side), but I like the maximum size and resolution (800×800). Save them no larger than 800×800 pixels or eBay will resize them back to 400×400. I suggest you save them in JPEG format (.jpg) to match eBay's picture protocol. You can also use .bmp, .gif, .tif, and .png formats, but I have found the fewest problems with .jpg.

8.17   **"How many pictures should I use in a listing?"**

For familiar items that most buyers would recognize, one or two pictures are usually sufficient. For collectibles, I like to take 6 to 10 pictures. Take full-length pictures then add macro shots of the most important or attractive part of the item, such as the pattern on dishes, or the face or clothing of a doll. Take a picture of any certificate of authenticity, numbered edition, or autograph.

8.18 "Can I use a scanner instead of a camera?"

Yes. In fact, a scanner works very well on all types of flat items such as books, baseball cards, comic books, and coins. I have even produced a good picture of products sealed in flat blister packs.

A scanner actually gives a color-rich picture and has fewer problems with glare. One problem is that a scanner produces a very large file. Therefore, before you scan the item, use the menu and resize the resolution to 72 dpi. That quality is fine for eBay yet produces a much smaller file size.

POWERSELLER TIP

Sometimes a scanner can produce an annoying moiré pattern. If this happens, see question 8.11.

8.19 "What does white balance mean?"

It is when you adjust the light control on your camera to match the light sources in your room. Digital cameras today try to automatically adjust to the light in a room to give the item the proper hue. However, most rooms where you will be taking the photos will have three sources of light; the overhead room light, the light from the window, and any extra photography lights you set up. Sometimes the camera is confused by the different light sources and chooses the wrong source. This produces an incorrect color or tint to your item instead of the true color.

To correct this problem, use the menu on your camera to set the white balance of the camera. The way to accomplish this is to set everything up for the shot including all the light sources. Now just before you snap the picture, place a white piece of paper in front of the item and select the custom white balance feature on your camera. You have just told the camera, "Based on all the light sources in the room, this paper is white." The camera then discerns what should be white and adjusts its settings accordingly. The result is a picture of your item with its true color.

8.20 "Can I copy a picture from a manufacturer's website?"

Not unless you have the manufacturer's permission. If you are an authorized reseller of their products, they will most likely grant permission, but always ask first.

8.21 "Can I copy a picture from another seller's listing?"

Never copy a picture from a seller's listing without her permission. You could get into some pretty heated e-mail exchanges if you do this. If the seller decides to report you to eBay, you could be in a lot of trouble, including possible suspension.

Take your own picture and make it different from the other sellers'. Distinguish yourself and your listing. Some sellers all use the same stock gallery photo from the manufacturer, so no one listing stands out from the others. Mix it up. If all your competition is using the same stock picture in their gallery photos, take a picture of the box or blister pack. Now your listing will be the one that stands out from all those "professional" pictures.

8.22 "How do I keep other sellers from stealing my picture?"

Watermark them. They can still copy the photo but there is no reason to, because you just placed your brand on the photo. When you watermark an item, you place a faint image on the picture such as your name or logo. The watermark is not so visible as to disfigure the picture, but it's visible enough to keep anyone from using your photo in their listings.

Watermarking is definitely advisable if you sell artwork. Without question, do this if it is your own artwork. Most of the photo-editing software today offers watermarking features.

9 Domestic Shipping

One of the most important, yet sometimes least considered, components of eBay selling is shipping. Just because shipping is the last step in the overall process doesn't mean in any way that it should not be thought about or considered until the last minute. Shipping costs have a direct effect on your overall profit.

Shipping Carriers

Most eBay sellers use the USPS, UPS, FedEx, or DHL as their shipping carrier. Each provides different services, conveniences, and fees. This chapter will present the most common shipping questions and problems eBay sellers have when using these carriers.

9.1 "Do you recommend UPS, FedEx, DHL, or USPS for domestic shipping?"

This is entirely your decision and should be based on what rate is cheapest for the type of items you sell and the easiest for home pick-up or drop-off at their counters. There is no one-size-fits-all answer. I ship some items by UPS and FedEx, but most are sent by the United States Postal Service (USPS).

I spent considerable time researching domestic and international shipping rates, as well as packaging options. I will provide a summary of my findings and a flow chart to help you make quick but informed shipping decisions. For more detailed information about shipping for eBay sellers, please refer to my book *eBay Business at Your Fingertips*.

Domestic Shipping Decision Chart

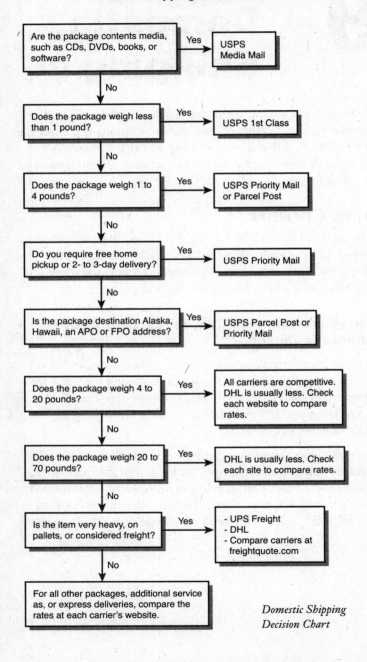

Are the package contents media, such as CDs, DVDs, books, or software? → **Yes** → USPS Media Mail

↓ No

Does the package weigh less than 1 pound? → **Yes** → USPS 1st Class

↓ No

Does the package weigh 1 to 4 pounds? → **Yes** → USPS Priority Mail or Parcel Post

↓ No

Do you require free home pickup or 2- to 3-day delivery? → **Yes** → USPS Priority Mail

↓ No

Is the package destination Alaska, Hawaii, an APO or FPO address? → **Yes** → USPS Parcel Post or Priority Mail

↓ No

Does the package weigh 4 to 20 pounds? → **Yes** → All carriers are competitive. DHL is usually less. Check each website to compare rates.

↓ No

Does the package weigh 20 to 70 pounds? → **Yes** → DHL is usually less. Check each site to compare rates.

↓ No

Is the item very heavy, on pallets, or considered freight? → **Yes** → - UPS Freight / - DHL / - Compare carriers at freightquote.com

↓ No

For all other packages, additional service as, or express deliveries, compare the rates at each carrier's website.

Domestic Shipping Decision Chart

Use the chart on the previous page as a guideline, but also spend some time on all of the carriers' websites comparing prices for shipping the particular items that you sell. Your decision will be based on the size, weight, destination, insurance, and any other services required. Note that the flow chart assumes you are shipping the item in a small to standard-size box, and the chart is to be used as a quick guide. When sending large, oversized, or heavy boxes, double-check all details and restrictions on the website of the carrier you will use.

USPS

The United States Postal Service (USPS) usually tops all other carriers for small, lightweight packages (under 2 lbs) or for packages to neighboring destinations (within the same state). USPS rates are also competitive with FedEx and UPS for ground deliveries.

Pros:

- Free Priority Mail boxes.
- Flat rates and free Flat Rate Priority Mail boxes.
- Priority Mail is delivered in two to three days.
- Free home pick-up (at least one package must be Priority Mail).
- Much cheaper rates for shipments to Alaska.
- Saturday deliveries.
- Delivers to PO Boxes.
- Delivers to APO/FPO addresses (military overseas).
- Free APO/FPO Flat Rate Priority Mail boxes (with a rate $2 cheaper than using a standard Flat Rate box).
- No extra charge for rural or remote deliveries.
- Multiple, convenient drop-off service counters.
- Considerable discount when shipping by media mail.
- The same Priority Mail boxes can be used for international shipments (so less boxes to store).
- Free Delivery Confirmation if postage is purchased online.

Cons:

- Not a good choice for heavier items or freight.
- Does not include $100 insurance or true tracking throughout journey (only final Delivery Confirmation).

UPS

United Parcel Service (UPS) is competitive with other carriers in the 4–70-pound range.

Pros:

- Competitive for very heavy items or freight when using their freight service.
- UPS provides multiple, convenient drop-off locations when including their partners such as Staples and Office Depot.
- Offers a Special Pricing Program of discounted shipping and home pick-up rates to eBay sellers.
- Includes $100 insurance and true tracking.

Cons:

- Least competitive for items weighing 2–10 pounds.
- Free boxes are available for Express shipments only.
- Charges $3 per package for home pick-up.
- Does not deliver to PO boxes.
- Adds a fee for Saturday deliveries.
- Not a good choice for Alaska shipments.

FedEx

Federal Express (FedEx) offers competitive rates with USPS and UPS for ground shipments between 4 and 70 pounds.

Pros:

- Competitive for packages 4–70 pounds.
- Competitive for heavy ground shipments.
- Competitive for freight shipments.

- Convenient drop-off counters (Kinko's).
- Includes $100 insurance and true tracking.

Cons:

- Charges $3 per package for home pick-up.
- Does not deliver to PO boxes.
- Free boxes are available for Express shipments only.
- Adds a fee for Saturday deliveries.
- Not a good choice for Alaska shipments.

DHL

DHL (the last-name initials of the three founders) usually offers the lowest rates for standard ground shipments but is not as convenient for drop-off locations throughout the nation when compared with all other carriers.

Pros:

- Usually the lowest rates for standard ground shipments.
- Excellent rates to businesses for heavy or freight shipments.
- Includes $100 insurance and true tracking.

Cons:

- Charges $3 per pick-up for home pick-up (compared to $3 per package for FedEx and UPS).
- Does not deliver to PO boxes.
- Free boxes are available for Express shipments only.
- Adds a fee for Saturday deliveries.
- Not a good choice for Alaska shipments.

Learn more about shipping items with USPS, UPS, FedEx, or DHL from the following links:

- USPS at http://pages.ebay.com/usps/home.html
- UPS at http://pages.ebay.com/ups/SellerSolutions.html
- FedEx at www.fedex.com
- DHL at www.dhl.com

9.2 "Which carrier do you use?"

The USPS usually works best for me, because most of the items I sell fit nicely in their free Priority Mail boxes. This may not be true for the items you sell. However, if your items do fit in the boxes, think about the savings with using free boxes. Even if you ship small items, a box from an office supply store will probably cost around $3. If you ship five items a day, that is $450 a month!

SEE ALSO 9.9 "How do I get those free co-branded eBay/USPS Priority Mail boxes?"

9.3 "Doesn't Priority Mail cost more than UPS or Parcel Post?"

Not as much as you may think for packages under 4 pounds. In most cases the difference between Parcel Post and Priority Mail is less than $2 depending on the destination. You just charge the extra amount in your shipping rate. There are some real advantages in using Priority Mail:

- Free Priority Mail boxes.

- Two- or three-day delivery time coast-to-coast, compared with seven to ten days for Parcel Post or other carriers.

- Fewer lost or damaged packages compared to using Parcel Post or UPS (based on my experience).

- You can state in your description that you ship by Priority Mail.

- Free home pick-up. You must have at least one package that is shipped by Priority Mail to qualify for free home pick-up.

- Excellent feedback received because of such quick deliveries.

Certainly not every item I sell needs to be shipped by Priority Mail. Small and lightweight items under 1 pound can be mailed in bubble-pack envelopes and sent First Class. I send all media items such as books, software, CDs, and DVDs by USPS Media Mail. However, if the items need to be shipped in a box or need to arrive sooner, I check to see if they will fit in a free Priority Mail box.

Pre-Paid Postage and Home Pick-Up

9.4 "How can I schedule a home pick-up from the carriers?"

First, you will need to set up an account with the carrier of your choice. Then search their website for "home pick-up."

The pick-up rates from the different carriers are provided in the table below. Note that the USPS provides free pick-up but all other carriers charge a pick-up or package rate. For a free USPS carrier pick-up, remember that at least one package needs to be mailed by Priority Mail. If you require daily pick-ups, contact the carrier for their variable rates that are dependant on volume.

Home Pick-Up Comparison Chart	
Carrier	Pick-Up Fee
USPS Parcel Post	Free with 1 Priority Mail package
USPS Priority Mail	Free
UPS	$3 per package
FedEx	$3 per package
DHL	$3 per pick-up

Before you choose home pick-up, there is one important question to consider: do you feel comfortable placing all of your items outside your front door where they will sit until the carrier stops by? If not, see the next two questions.

9.5 "What if I don't want to leave the packages on my porch or wait in line at the post office?"

You can use your My eBay page to easily pay for and print the postage. Then drop off the pre-paid packages at the post office. See the next question.

9.6 "How do I print pre-paid postage for either drop-off or home pick-up?"

Go to your My eBay page and select your Sold items to see a list of all items you have recently sold. Click on the **Print Shipping Label** button next to the winning bidder's name. You will be rerouted to PayPal for login. You will then see the particular transaction you have selected. PayPal knows the item, your shipping method, your address, and the address of the recipient. You then pay for the shipping with a few mouse clicks, and print the pre-paid postage on a standard sheet of paper.

Use clear packing tape to attach the pre-paid postage shipping label to the box. When you go to the post office you just drop them off at their counter or in their package drop bin. There is no need to wait because the postage is already paid and attached. Just drop and go.

Your receipt for the postage is in your PayPal account. This is a great way to avoid long lines during the Christmas season. Note that if you have several packages a day, your USPS clerk may require that you bring the packages to her loading dock. This is often even quicker for you, because you just drive up and unload your parcels. You don't even need to find a parking space most of the time.

SEE ALSO **Appendix A "A Complete Order-Fulfillment Process"**

Tracking, Delivery Confirmation, and Insurance

9.7 "Do you suggest paying for tracking when shipping items?"

Not usually. FedEx, UPS, and DHL provide tracking at no extra charge. USPS provides Delivery Confirmation free of charge when shipping is purchased online.

Be sure you understand the difference between "tracking" and "Delivery Confirmation." DHL, UPS, and FedEx provide actual tracking so you know where your package is at each waypoint throughout its transit. If the package is held up for any reason, you are able to find it. That's not what the USPS offers with Delivery Confirmation.

The USPS will only confirm when the package has been delivered. That's why it's called Delivery Confirmation and not tracking. If the item is lost or late, you cannot find it from their website.

However, you need Delivery Confirmation in order to qualify for PayPal Seller Protection. Therefore, purchase and print pre-paid shipping labels online with PayPal (see question 9.6) from the USPS, and you will receive free Delivery Confirmation for Priority Mail packages. For all First Class, Media Mail, and Parcel Post packages, you will need to purchase Delivery Confirmation. Understand also that any item worth over $250 needs Signature Confirmation to qualify for PayPal Seller Protection.

SEE ALSO **1.34** **"What is PayPal's Seller Protection Program?"**

9.8 "Do you purchase insurance when you ship items?"

It depends mostly on the value of the item and how fragile it is. Remember that FedEx, UPS, and DHL offer $100 of insurance free of charge. If the item is worth more than that amount, I usually purchase additional insurance.

When I use the USPS, if the item is under $100 and the address is "confirmed" by PayPal, then I usually do not purchase insurance. If the item is expensive or breakable, I will purchase insurance. If it is worth over $250, I also require a Signature Confirmation. Be sure to include the additional costs in your shipping charges when you list the item.

Here is something to remember about purchasing insurance for inexpensive items. I ship smaller items by the USPS. In my experience, the USPS rarely loses a package. It may be late (sometimes really late), but eventually it seems to get there. A few years ago I noticed how much money I was spending on insurance for smaller packages and the number of claims made. I was spending a lot of money for nothing. It was a clear business decision for me to let the inexpensive items (less than $100) go without insurance and keep my money. If a customer says it never arrived, I ship another item or refund his money. With this decision, at the end of the year I am always ahead.

POWERSELLER TIP

Consider using a third-party insurer such as U-Pic or DSI to save costs. You can even charge USPS insurance rates to the buyer but then purchase it yourself from U-Pic or DSI and make a 50 percent profit on the insurance cost. To learn more, go to www.u-pic.com and www.dsiinsurance.com.

Corrugated Boxes and Packing Materials

9.9 "How do I get those free co-branded eBay/USPS Priority Mail boxes?"

The USPS loves eBay sellers. They have even teamed with eBay in order to provide co-branded Priority Mail boxes. The boxes are stamped with phrases such as "Buy it on eBay. Ship it with the U.S. Postal Service."

There are currently four different sizes of variable-weight co-branded boxes and two sizes of flat rate. You can order the boxes in quantities of 10 or 25 and place an order for each box size once a day. There is no charge for the boxes or for shipment to you. It is indeed free and a great deal. Order the co-branded boxes from http://ebaysupplies.usps.com.

9.10 "Where can I get corrugated boxes, padded envelopes, and other packing materials at a reasonable price?"

Purchasing corrugated boxes from office supply stores is an expensive choice. A box from these sources at retail prices is usually much higher than the cost from corrugated box suppliers when purchased in bulk. This has a direct and significant impact on your bottom line.

For example, consider a seller who has a part-time eBay business selling five items a day. The required shipping boxes cost $5.00 each from an office supply store, but only 75¢ from a corrugated box supplier. That is a savings of over $21.25 per day ($4.25 × 5) or a surprising $637.50 per month ($21.25 × 30 days).

To find corrugated boxes in your area, go to www.thomasnet.com or search the Internet using the keywords "corrugated box" in your state. I personally use and recommend Uline at www.uline.com.

Uline offers everything you will ever need for boxes and mailers. They have locations strategically placed around the country. Their prices are usually so reasonable that even when you include the cost of shipping the boxes to you, they are still much cheaper than using local corrugated box suppliers.

I suggest you purchase boxes in quantities of 50, 100, or more in order to receive the best discounted pricing. The boxes will be sent to you in flat stacks for cheaper shipping and easy storage.

Check the Uline website from time to time to see if the boxes you use are on sale. When they are, you can order boxes at just a fraction of the price that office supply stores charge. As an example, there is a certain box I use that costs a hefty $6 at the local office supply store. My unit cost when I order 100 boxes, including shipping the boxes to me, is a mere 70¢!

9.11 "Do you also purchase your packing materials online?"

Not usually. It is too costly to have large quantities of bulk packing materials such as bubble wrap or Styrofoam peanuts shipped. I usually reuse packing materials from the shipments I receive from my product wholesalers or I get them from local merchants of gift, hardware, or furniture stores. Ask them if you can have their packing materials.

Don't forget about eBay. Many times eBay sellers discover after an exhaustive online search that some of the best prices for their boxes, mailers, and packing materials are on eBay. In addition, shipping supplies such as tape, tape dispensers, shipping labels, shipping box dividers, and rubber stamps are all found on eBay. Just watch the seller's shipping rates to ensure it is still a good deal.

9.12 "Do you also reuse shipping boxes?"

Only if they are in good condition. Many eBay sellers reuse shipping boxes, cut them down to a new shape, and use black markers to cross out the printing.

Reusing a box is okay in my opinion as long as the box is not damaged or there are no labels still attached. Remember, the box is the very first impression of your service to your buyer. A box that has labels and printing blacked out, or too much packing tape that was not fully removed, gives an unprofessional impression. It could be a determining factor for a meager or even poor feedback comment.

9.13 "What type of packing material do you recommend?"

I've tried several and there are pros and cons for each type. First, let's discuss the packing material to avoid for general merchandise items: those soft Styrofoam peanuts or shredded newspaper. Why? Because it upsets many of your customers having to pick up all those clingy peanuts or newspaper shreds.

If your item is breakable (such as glassware), I recommend bubble wrap around the glass with newspaper stuffed inside the glass. The rest of the package can be cushioned with loosely crumpled newspaper. If, however, it's an expensive item (I hate to say this), then use Styrofoam peanuts. The goal is to not have the item shift. For expensive items, consider double-boxing with sufficient cushioning in both boxes.

If you can't find a local supplier of inexpensive packing materials, consider visiting local retailers. This is another way the act of recycling can be passed along. You can get free bubble wrap at stores such as Hallmark, Radio Shack, hardware stores, or almost any store that sells small or fragile items. Furniture stores have large bubble wrap or other packing material on each piece of furniture they receive.

Also in the spirit of recycling, check out www.freecycle.org. It is a free Yahoo! group that has "boards" for different locations. You can place a want ad for free packing supplies in your area and find local sources.

For most nonbreakable, prepackaged (in their own packaging) general merchandise items, I recommend newspaper. Lightly crumple one sheet of newspaper. Don't make it too tight or there won't be as much cushion during shipment. Place lightly crumpled newspaper sheets on the bottom of the box, more around the sides of the item, and on top. Gently shake the box to ensure the item does not shift. Then your item should be safe and secure inside the box.

If you have an item that is not prepackaged, such as clothing, then you risk getting newspaper ink on the item. To prevent this, seal the item in a plastic bag. A wide variety of clear, white, or opaque bags can be purchased at grocery, hardware, or discount stores.

So the next time you're asked to sign up for your local newspaper, your answer should be, "Yes, sign me up!" It is a legitimate business write-off. You can decide whether or not you read the paper. Meanwhile, you will have fresh packing material delivered to your driveway each morning.

Other popular packing materials include plastic air bags. Some eBay shippers even create their own by blowing into a freezer bag and sealing it. Be careful when using very thin plastic bags—excessive heat or cold during transit can deflate or even pop the bags. For this reason, I don't use them for breakable items.

If you would prefer to use clean white paper for a more professional packing presentation, consider butcher paper or industrial tissue from a local source or Uline. Moving companies also sell white packing paper. Visit your local newspaper and ask if you can either have (for free) or possibly purchase their "end rolls." If you cannot find a local source for bubble wrap, try uline.com, papermart.com, fast-pack.com, or eBay.

Packing Tips

9.14 "How should I pack my items so they will arrive safely?"

You cannot guarantee safe delivery because half of the determining factor is how the package is handled during transit. However, there are certain packing guidelines that, when followed, should minimize damage during shipping.

Boxes:

- Use durable shipping boxes with no punctures, tears, or corner dents and with all flaps intact.
- Do not exceed the gross weight limit for the box. This is usually displayed in the "box certificate" that is stamped on one of the bottom flaps. For heavier items, use double-wall boxes.

Packing Materials:

- Less expensive and nonbreakable items can be wrapped in a variety of packing materials including newspaper.

- Expensive or breakable items should be packed in bubble wrap and placed in Styrofoam peanuts. Large bubble wrap should be used for breakable items because the smaller bubbles do not provide adequate protection.

- Use Styrofoam peanuts to pack trinkets, lamps, fine china, figurines, and other breakable items. Peanuts can settle or allow the item to settle during transit. Therefore use at least 3 inches of peanuts around the item and then completely fill the box to the top. Jiggle the box gently to settle the peanuts and refill.

- Use 2–3 inches of cushioning packing material on the bottom, all sides, and the top to ensure the item does not shift during transit. Close the box and gently shake it to ensure that there is minimal movement.

- When shipping very fragile items, use two or three layers of different packing materials, and possibly double-box the item.

- When shipping multiple items in one box, wrap each item individually and place additional packing material between the items.

- Use inflatable air bags only for lightweight items that do not have sharp corners or edges. As mentioned earlier, do not use air bags for expensive items. The bags can break, shrink, or burst from extreme hot or cold temperatures.

- Use pressure-sensitive or nylon-reinforced 2-inch or wider tape that is specifically made to seal shipping boxes. Do not use cellophane tape, masking tape, duct tape, electrical tape, or string. Tape the box end to end on both the top and bottom flaps.

- For heavy items, seal with heavy-duty or reinforced tape. Apply additional tape to the bottom of the box, as it will bear the weight. Once the box is closed, seal the box by placing additional tape on the top- and bottom-edge seams.

9.15 "How do you ship books?"

If it is a valuable, autographed, or rare first-edition book, I ship it in a Priority Mail box to protect it during shipping. Of course the buyer pays for the extra cost of the shipping. If the book is very heavy or you are shipping several books, you may want to use one of the Flat Rate Priority Mail boxes for $8.95 or $12.95. Be sure to mention how you will ship the book in your item description to justify higher shipping and handling costs.

For all other books, I ship them in heavily padded envelopes or corrugated boxes using the USPS Media Mail rate. If the book is heavy, Media Mail is substantially cheaper than Priority Mail or Parcel Post. Remember, when selecting the padded envelopes, they need to be thick enough to sufficiently protect the edges of the book. You don't want bad feedback because of poor packaging that resulted in a damaged book corner. If in doubt, use a box.

Media Mail used to take a few weeks but now it usually takes about a week to 10 days. Be sure to mention in your shipping description "In order to save you money on shipping, the book will be shipped by Media Mail and should take a minimum of 7–10 days."

POWERSELLER TIP

Media Mail includes books, manuscripts, CDs, DVDs, and film. It does not, however, include magazines. You cannot place any marketing or advertising material along with a Media Mail shipment. Also, understand that if you are ever tempted to send something by Media Mail that does not qualify as media, the postal clerk has every right to open a Media Mail package to verify its contents. This could be an embarrassing development for you. You will get to know your postal clerk very well as an eBay seller. Stick to the rules.

If it is getting close to Christmas, it would be best to ship the books by Priority Mail. Media Mail or Parcel Post may not make it there in time. You will have some anxious customers e-mailing you every other day, and you don't need that pressure.

Some books are small, thin, or lightweight. If the book and the padded mailing envelope is less than 1 pound, ship it First Class. Often it is just a few cents more (and sometimes even cheaper) to ship it First Class rather than Media Mail.

POWERSELLER TIP

If you are shipping books in an envelope, you still need to avoid the risk of a damaged corner. Use two pieces of cardboard slightly bigger than the book and sandwich the book inside. You can even use plastic wrap to tightly wrap around the cardboard pieces securing the book inside.

9.16 "How do you ship CDs or other items that are small, lightweight, flat, and not really breakable?"

I use a bubble-padded envelope specifically made for CDs and mail it First Class or Media Mail. Be sure, however, that the item is not breakable. If that is not the case, ship it by Priority Mail in their free box designed to ship VHS tapes (available at your local post office). Alternatively, if you ship many of these types of items, purchase your own corrugated boxes from Uline at www.uline.com and ship them First Class or Media Mail.

9.17 "How can I ship large items or freight?"

Well, first, there are two things you can do when you create the listing to avoid the hassle altogether. In the shipping section of the Sell Your Item form, you can choose "For local pick-up only." This means your customer needs to be in your locale or vicinity and would have to pick up the item at your home or office. This certainly limits your potential bidders.

You can also state in your description that the buyer is responsible to arrange for shipping. This now takes you out of the loop, and if something goes wrong during delivery, he can't blame you.

UPS Freight

If you need to arrange the shipping, you have several choices among the major carriers. Did you know that UPS and DHL have freight services? I have used them several times. Their rates are usually much lower than the cost of using major trucking lines.

This is a funny story. I once received a quote from a major trucking line to ship three pallets of product from Denver to Seattle. I then got a quote from UPS freight. UPS was half the cost. Guess what truck pulled up to deliver the pallets? The same trucking company that had quoted twice the rate! UPS had subcontracted the delivery to the major trucking line. By using UPS freight, I received the same quality service from a major trucking line but at half the price.

I suggest you call UPS and DHL freight and receive a quote. Then compare their quotes with the major trucking lines using Freightquote. com.

Freightquote.com

Freightquote.com provides small businesses with free, quick comparison quotes for freight services among all carriers. This service is similar to travel comparison sites that search for the best airline, hotel, and car rental prices. A shipper simply completes the information online, and Freightquote.com returns a rate comparison for all relevant trucking lines. There is no charge to use their service because the trucking line that wins your business will pay the Freightquote. com fees.

Uship.com

Uship.com is a shipping website that provides Auction-Style listings and quotes for shipping larger items. You create a listing with your shipment details and then receive shipping quotes from various shippers. Savings can sometimes reach 50 to 60 percent off standard trucking-line rates when quoted separately.

9.18 "Do you purchase insurance for freight?"

Yes, but not with the major carriers. I use private insurance companies such as DSI and U-Pic to insure freight shipments. Typical savings can be 50 percent off the standard trucking-line rates. Compare their services and rates here:

- www.u-pic.com
- www.dsiinsurance.com

Delivery Problems

9.19   "My customer says she never received my Priority Mail package. It has been more than a week. What should I do?"

Be patient. With some luck it should be there shortly. The USPS can usually deliver a Priority Mail package across the country in two to three days, but that is not a guarantee. Sometimes a package is delayed for a few more days. This is especially true during the Christmas season.

I would estimate that this happens to me once in every 80 shipments. What I have learned is that, in almost every case, just about the time the customer was on the verge of panic, the package arrived within the next day or two. Again, this has happened almost every time— even after a hurricane in Florida destroyed my customer's post office (it was two weeks late).

Lesson learned: don't panic. The USPS will almost always get it there eventually. What you need to do when you get the panic e-mail is to buy some time. I suggest you send an e-mail to your customer with a reassuring message such as the following:

Dear [Customer's First Name],

Thank you for bringing this matter to my attention. I checked our records and we packed and shipped your item on [Date] by USPS Priority Mail. Usually, Priority Mail is very fast and will get the package to you within two to three days. So yes, it should have arrived by now.

Although rare, sometimes the USPS does deliver their Priority Mail packages late. When this has happened in the past, in almost every case, the package ended up arriving just a few days later. So I think the best thing we can do right now is to wait a few more days.

It is unfortunate that the USPS is late delivering your package, but be assured we did indeed ship it on the above date. It should be there very shortly. Your patience during this waiting period is appreciated.

Please let me know as soon as it arrives. If, however, it still has not arrived by [date], please contact me again.

Thank you again for your purchase!

Sincerely,

[Your Name]

[Your Company Name]

That is a very reassuring e-mail. What more can you do and what more can he expect from you (assuming he is reasonable)? When he receives the package, he will see that you did indeed ship it on the date you indicated. With your quick and reassuring communication, you should still receive good feedback from him.

If, however, the package still doesn't arrive within another three to four business days, you need to take further action. See the next question.

POWERSELLER TIP

You will need to respond to a panic e-mail from time to time. I suggest you write and save the preceding response letter in a Word document. When your customer sends you a shipping panic e-mail, you simply copy/paste this answer, change the name and date, and hit send.

9.20 "My customer claims she never received my package. It has been nearly two weeks. What should I do?"

This has happened to me a few times when I used UPS and FedEx, twice on international shipments, and a few more times with domestic USPS delivery. When it does, I check the buyer's feedback just to be sure other sellers aren't complaining about phony claims of non-delivery. Otherwise, I always assume the customer is honest and the package was indeed lost.

If you shipped the item with FedEx, UPS, and DHL you will have a tracking number and can usually track down the package to determine the problem. Most of the time, the address makes the package undeliverable. Sometimes it is an error in the carrier's computer system. The address is correct but for some reason their computer is telling them there is no such address.

What I suggest is to find out as much information as possible from their tracking website, then call the carrier and speak with a live representative. Whatever the problem is, you know where the package is and where the buyer lives, so you will be able to solve the problem.

POWERSELLER TIP

One time, after a few go-arounds with a FedEx representative, I had to get creative. The rep insisted his computer was correct and the package was not deliverable to a certain address. I guess he thought that the buyer didn't really know his own home address. I finally gave up and had the package shipped to the buyer's work. You could also have it shipped to his friend or neighbor.

There is one catch to this problem if you are using a drop shipper. The carrier won't deal with you. They will only deal with the shipper or recipient. There is no way around this. You will need to get the drop shipper involved with the carrier to solve the problem.

SEE ALSO **12.15** "What is a drop shipper?"

If you shipped the package by USPS, even with Delivery Confirmation, you won't know where it is or why it is being delayed. Eventually it should be delivered to the customer or returned to you. Meanwhile, you need to fix the problem.

If the item is not one of a kind, and is relatively inexpensive, then ship the buyer another item with UPS. Be sure to purchase Signature Confirmation and pay for it online with PayPal. Using UPS, you will now be able to track the second package. Adding Signature Confirmation makes it nearly impossible to claim nonreceipt.

If you purchased insurance and tracking, file a claim for nonreceipt with the carrier. Remember also that for the first package, because you paid for the shipping with PayPal, you may qualify for PayPal Seller Protection if the buyer claims nonreceipt. Be sure to file a claim with PayPal to get your money refunded for the item and shipping.

SEE ALSO   1.34 *"What is PayPal's Seller Protection Program?"*

If you sent a one-of-a-kind item, I would apologize and refund her money. I would also e-mail the PayPal mail receipt or scan the USPS receipt showing the date it was shipped to her zip code and e-mail it to her. Those two actions should keep you from getting bad feedback.

I would rather have a reputation for great customer service. If you have to send a duplicate item or spend time informing your buyer about what has happened, consider it part of the cost of doing business. Those customers will probably make more purchases. Hopefully you can make up for your loss on this item with your next sale to her.

9.21 "How do I file a claim if my package gets lost or is damaged?"

You should contact the carrier immediately to determine the specific claim process for the package or item. For damaged goods, the carrier will usually return to the customer's home, pick up the item, and take it to their central office for examination and a refund decision. For the USPS, the customer usually has to take it to the post office.

Even with irrefutable evidence of rough handling (torn or crushed packages), the particular carrier can also claim that the item was not properly cushioned or packed. Therefore, if it is obvious that the item has been damaged, it is best to have your customer not fully unpack the package. Instead, leave the item wrapped in the packing material to show that it was indeed packaged properly.

As much as possible, you should be the one to deal with the carrier. Take the customer out of the claims loop, refund her money, or send a replacement. Deal with the carrier separately. Although this is inconvenient, it is part of being an online retailer.

The best solution is to avoid potential damage as much as possible. Pack the item securely in a proper shipping box. This will minimize breakage and maximize the chance for refund approval from the carrier.

SEE ALSO   9.14 *"How should I pack my items so they will arrive safely?"*

Shipping Rates

9.22 "How can I determine how much to charge for shipping?"

The first decision you need to make is, will you be charging a flat rate or using eBay's automatic shipping calculator? According to eBay statistics, most customers prefer a flat rate. When you use a calculated rate, if they are not logged in to eBay, they now may have to enter their zip code to see their rate, and it is just more clicks they have to perform to get the answer.

When a buyer does a keyword search, your listing will appear along with several others. If most sellers provide a shipping rate and you require the buyer to enter his zip code, it is quite likely he will skip right over your listing. Therefore, choosing a flat rate over a calculated rate is a good marketing decision when practical. Note that when buyers are logged in to their eBay account, however, eBay performs this calculation automatically. Because most eBay buyers are logged in when they search, it would usually be a small number of potential bidders who would be affected.

POWERSELLER TIP

EBay restricts sellers to maximum shipping charges on books, DVDs and movies, CDs, and music and video games. To learn more, select the **Help** link and type **Maximum Shipping and Handling Costs**.

I have also noticed on many eBay Seller discussion boards that sometimes eBay, the USPS, or UPS gets the calculated rate wrong. That is another reason to avoid using the calculated rate.

There are times, however, when you need to use the calculated rate. Personally, I use a flat rate for items under about 5 pounds and a calculated rate for items that weigh over 5 pounds. The reason is that for heavier items, it is not fair to charge the same flat rate to a local customer that a distant customer has to pay (unless I'm shipping using a flat-rate Priority Mail box, where the cost is the same either way).

How to Determine a Shipping Rate

First, you need to establish the total weight of the item, package, and packing material as follows:

- Have your item fully packed and in the box as if ready to ship.

- Use your digital postal scale and note the weight.

Here's how to determine a flat rate for domestic shipments (to the 48 states):

- Assuming you are shipping by USPS, go to http://ircalc.usps. gov.

- Select the United States as your country, select **package,** and enter the weight and your zip code. Now enter the destination zip code in a small town in the United States that is the farthest away from you. (Hint, go to http://zip4.usps.com/zip4/ citytown.jsp to look up zip codes by city.)

- Select **Continue.**

- Select the way you will ship the item (Express, Priority, Parcel Post, or Media Mail).

- Select any extra services (such as Delivery Confirmation or Insurance) or if none, select **Continue.**

- Your total shipping rate is provided.

- Add any handling charge (I suggest no more than $2 unless the box is expensive).

- You now have your flat shipping rate to anywhere in the 48 states. You will use this rate later when you create the listing for this item.

Here's how to determine a flat rate for international shipments:

- Assuming you are shipping by USPS, go to http://ircalc.usps.gov.

- Select the destination country, select package, enter the weight, and select **Continue.**

- Select the method of shipment (Global Express Guaranteed, Express Mail International, Priority Mail International, or First Class Mail International).

- Select any extra services.
- Your total international shipping rate is provided.
- Add any handling charge (I suggest no more than $3).
- You now have the flat standard shipping rate to that country.

If you want eBay to calculate the rate for either domestic or international shipments, here's how:

- During listing creation, on the Shipping page, select **Shipping Calculator.**
- Enter the weight, carrier, method of shipment and handling charge, and any additional services.
- Your buyer can now receive his shipping rate by clicking the **Calculate** link in your listing and entering his zip code. If he is logged in, eBay performs this calculation automatically.

POWERSELLER TIP

The USPS also has flat rates to different countries. The rate depends on the weight of the package, so check to see if a flat rate or variable weight postage is best for your international packages.

9.23 "Do you charge a handling fee? If yes, how much?"

Yes, I believe it is acceptable to charge a reasonable handling fee. EBay is a form of an online mail-order business. Such businesses add handling charges in order to cover the packaging effort and materials.

I usually charge $2 per package. If the package contains multiple items, I still only charge $2. I charge a $3 handling charge for international shipments. It only takes an extra minute to complete a Customs Declaration Form. Note that you should spell out "Shipping and Handling" rather than "S&H" in your descriptions, or you will receive e-mails from international buyers wanting to know what S&H means (for example, in the UK it's called Postage and Packing or P&P).

One quick way to eBay extinction is to overcharge your customers for shipping. You have too much competition. You should charge just enough to cover your costs, not make significant additional profit. Simply add $2 to the actual rate, call everything Shipping and Handling in your description, and you are covered.

9.24 "What type of postal scale do you recommend and where can I get one?"

The one I use and recommend is the UltraShip 55, meaning it is rated for weights up to 55 pounds. These scales cost less, are better quality, and have more features than the postal scales sold by the USPS or in office supply stores. If you will be shipping heavier items, UltraShip also has scales for heavier weight ratings.

UltraShip Scale

The following are a few good features to keep in mind when deciding on a scale:

- It should have a digital readout.
- It should be able to display oz/lbs or g/kg (for international sales).
- You should be able to "zero" the readout. Sometimes you weigh envelopes, tubes, liquids, or other items that need to be placed in a holding container. Place the empty container on the scale, zero the readout, and then add the material. Now you know the weight of the liquid or material.
- It should have a "hold" feature to display the weight for several seconds after you remove the item. This is particularly helpful when large items on the scale cover the readout.
- A very good feature is to be able to physically separate the digital readout, and move it away from the scale for weighing items in a large box.
- It should be portable and run on batteries. You won't use the AC adaptor as much. As an eBay seller you are going to move that scale all over the house and garage. Get one that works with batteries.

All these features are available in the UltraShip scale. Keep in mind that there is nothing magical about the word "postal" in postal scale. It is a scale that weighs things. You can use this scale around the house to weigh items in the kitchen, garage, and basement. I routinely use mine to measure the weight of my fully packed suitcase so I don't exceed the 50-pound weight limit of the airlines.

As a comparison, the scales at the post office or office supply stores do not have nearly the features of the UltraShip scale. They are also considerably higher in price or lower in weight limits.

Finally, be very careful when purchasing these scales online—including eBay. Many sellers claim to be dealers when they are not. An unusually low price for a new scale is the tip-off that the dealer is not selling a genuine or new product. To avoid this common online fraud for my readers and eBay students, I began offering the Ultra-Ship 55 scales from my eBay Store, www.trainingu4auctions.net, or from my website, www.trainingu4auctions.com.

Other Shipping Questions

9.25 "Should I report a competitive seller for charging excessive shipping rates?"

I wouldn't if he is charging excessive shipping unless it is a "scam" sale. He won't be around very long and his listings make yours look like a good deal. I let these sellers' own greed weed them out of the marketplace.

If it is a scam sale, I report them. A scam sale is when a seller lists a small item at a fixed price of, say, 99¢ and then charges $35 for shipping (when it should be about $5). His eBay fees are based only on the 99¢. That is a scam against eBay and unfair to me as a seller as well, because I play by the rules and pay my fees. We don't need them in our community. The good news is that eBay is starting to crack down on these sellers—much to the applause of legitimate sellers who follow the rules.

To report a seller who has an exorbitant (scam) shipping charge, when viewing the listing page click the **Report item** link. Under the reason for report, select **Listing policy violations.** Under the detailed reason, select **Excessive shipping and handling.**

SEE ALSO **2.20** "I am interested in an item that is only $1, but the shipping charge is $35. The shipping should be about $5. What should I do?"

9.26 "I just sold multiple, different items to one buyer. However, eBay charged him full shipping for each item. What do I do?"

I immediately go to my PayPal account and send the buyer a refund. I also send her an e-mail explaining that eBay had overcharged for shipping and I just noticed it and gave her a refund. Do you think that customer is placing me on her "favorite seller list" and will be back for more items later?

Most multiple-item purchases are from a seller's eBay Store. You can solve this problem for future sales by using eBay's combined shipping discount service. See the next question.

9.27 "How can I offer a shipping discount for a multiple-item purchase?"

Sellers can use eBay's combined shipping discount service to offer shipping discounts for buyers who purchase multiple items.

This feature can be set up for both eBay's Flat Rate or Calculated Shipping Rate. You can also use your own custom discount rules based on each item's weight and size. Additionally, you can set promotional shipping discounts for purchases that total or exceed a designated sum.

Here's how to use eBay's combined shipping discount service:

1. Select the **Site Preferences** link under the My Account section on your My eBay page.

2. Click the **Show** link for **Shipping Preferences** and then click **Edit.**

3. Set up your discount rules as you desire. When buyers browse your items, they will now see messages automatically generated by eBay informing them of your combined shipping discounts.

9.28 "Do you include any type of materials in your shipping box?"

I like to at least include a copy of the packing slip. That contains all the details about the sale and becomes the buyer's receipt. I also include a thank-you letter and place it on top of all packing materials just before I seal the box. It will be the first thing the buyer sees when he opens the box.

The thank-you letter is a good first impression and highlights good customer service. Thank the customer for his purchase, encourage him to return for other purchases, and encourage him to leave you positive feedback.

You may also want to include coupons, business cards, or some other incentive to encourage repeat purchases. If you own an eBay Store, you can easily print readymade fliers and marketing materials for inclusion in the box.

SEE ALSO **11.13 "How do I market my store?"**

10 International Shipping

Shipping items to international customers takes a bit more effort than shipping domestically. However, that should not deter you from reaching a global market. Fortunately, it is very simple to ship small to medium-size packages overseas.

It's true that the cost to send a package to an international customer is more than to a domestic customer. However, my experience has been that international customers understand this and are accustomed to higher rates when ordering an item from the United States. If the item is a collectible or rare in their country, they are willing to pay more.

Also, with the current exchange rates, it is often more cost-effective for an international buyer to purchase from a U.S. seller and pay the higher shipping than it is to purchase the item in her own country.

Shipping Internationally with the USPS

10.1 "Which carrier is the best to use for international shipments?"

The United States Postal Service. For small to medium-size packages, the USPS rates are substantially lower than other carriers. For example, a 4-pound package sent by USPS Priority Mail International (PMI) to the UK would cost about $34. The same package sent by UPS, DHL, and FedEx would cost $85 to over $100!

International packages can be sent by the USPS using the following methods:

Express Mail International® (EMI). EMI offers a guaranteed "day certain" delivery to 190 countries. Automatic online tracking and $100 of insurance is included. The weight limit for EMI packages depends on the destination country.

Priority Mail® International (PMI). This accelerated airmail service is the way most small and lightweight packages should be sent. Use the free, domestic Priority Mail boxes up to 20 pounds, or you can send packages up to 70 pounds using your own box. Insurance and Delivery Confirmation is not included but can be purchased. See the next three questions for more information.

POWERSELLER TIP

Note that heavier or oversized items are sometimes cheaper to ship by EMI than PMI. Also, if you are shipping freight, then FedEx, UPS, and DHL are usually less than the USPS.

First-Class Mail® International (FCMI). This service has replaced Air Mail Parcel Post and surface mail (which is no longer available). Use FCMI to ship items under 4 pounds by air at a discounted rate.

M-Bags. These sacks are used to ship printed material such as books, magazines, and newspapers up to 66 pounds to international customers at a substantial discount. The items should be put in a box, and then place the box inside the M-Bag.

10.2 "Can I use the free Priority Mail boxes for international shipments?"

Yes. Priority Mail International packages can be sent to 190 countries with the same Priority Mail boxes used for domestic shipments. The restrictions are that the item will fit inside the box and the total package weighs 20 pounds or less. You can also use the Flat Rate Priority Mail boxes up to 20 pounds with a rate of $23 to Canada and Mexico and $38.95 to all other countries.

10.3 "How do I insure international packages?"

You can purchase insurance for international packages the same way as with domestic—online or counter. USPS offers optional insurance for damage or loss on packages shipped to most countries. A few samples of current international insurance rates are $1.95 for $50, $2.75 for $100, $3.80 for $200, and $6.95 for $500.

10.4 "How do I track international packages?"

True tracking is only available from USPS on their EMI packages. If you ship your items by PMI or FCMI, then you will not be able to track your package throughout its journey. You can only purchase Delivery Confirmation that will verify when the package has reached its destination. If you feel that your package needs tracking or notification of delivery that is better than Delivery Confirmation, then use EMI or consider sending the package as Registered Mail.

10.5 "Does the USPS provide home pick-up for international packages?"

Yes. You can schedule home pickup for international packages the same as you would for domestic packages. You can also print the required Customs Forms to attach to the packages.

SEE ALSO 9.4 "How can I schedule a home pick-up from the carriers?"

10.6 "Is it true that the USPS offers discounts for shipping internationally?"

The USPS has teamed with eBay to offer a discounted rate to sellers who purchase their international shipping labels online using PayPal. Priority Mail International (PMI) rates are discounted 5 percent and Express (EMI) rates 8 percent. To receive these discounts, go to your My eBay page and click on the **Print Shipping Label** link next to the name of your international customer. Follow the directions from there.

Customs Forms and Duty

10.7 "Do I have to charge or collect the Customs duty?"

No. It is the responsibility of the seller only to complete the Customs Declaration Forms correctly. You do not have to collect any additional duty (import tax). That is the responsibility of the Customs authorities in your customer's country.

10.8 "How does my international customer pay her duty and receive her packages?"

Every country has slightly different procedures for the collection of duty. Usually, however, all packages sent from the United States will first arrive at a foreign country's Customs office. A Customs officer will then assess the duty based on the information provided by the seller on the Customs Declaration Form. The officer has the right to open any package for further inspection or to verify its contents.

The package is then forwarded to your customer's local postal branch office and she is notified of its arrival. Your customer then pays for the assessed duty and is given the package.

10.9 "How do I complete the proper Customs forms?"

You can either complete the forms online or pick up the forms from your local post office. For items that are less than 4 pounds and can fit within a Priority Mail box, you should use Customs PS Form 2976 (sometimes known as the "short form"). This form is very simple to complete. All that is required is the sender's name and address, the recipient's name and address, a very brief description of the item, and the U.S. dollar value of the item.

Customs PS Form 2976

For items over 4 pounds or for any items sent First Class Mail International (FCMI), use Customs PS Form 2976-A. Be sure you check "Return to Sender" on the bottom right of the form in case the item is not deliverable. If that box is not checked, there is no guarantee it will be returned to you.

If you ship items by Express Mail International (EMI), you will need to complete Express Mailing Label 11-B as well as Customs Declaration PS Form 2976-A (sometimes called the "long form"). For additional questions about completing any of these forms, ask your USPS clerk, call 800-ASK-USPS, or visit the USPS website at www.usps.com.

10.10 **"My international customer wants me to change the information on the Customs form and mark it as a 'gift' or declare that the value is much less. Should I?"**

Do not be tempted to do this for your customer. You would be committing fraud. Remember that it is your name on the signature line, not your customer's. If you provide false information in order to avoid duty for your customer, you have committed fraud and, if caught, could be banned from ever selling to that country again. You will also be reported to the U.S. Attorney General's Office, who could level fines, or worse.

Send a simple and friendly e-mail to the buyer and write the following:

> "We acknowledge your desire to lower the duty, but please understand that we are a licensed, legitimate business in the state of [your state], in the United States. We must provide accurate international sales information and will not be able to accommodate your request to alter the Customs Form information. Thank you for your business."

If you receive several of these requests, you may want to add a disclaimer to your listings. State your policy clearly, briefly, and politely.

Other International Shipping Questions

10.11 "My winning bidder is international but I didn't want to ship outside the United States. What do I do?"

Unfortunately, eBay normally allows international buyers to bid on your item even when you indicate that you will only sell to the United States in your listing. You can correct this for future sales by setting your buyer requirement preferences properly. Once this is set, eBay will block anyone from bidding on your item who lives in a country where you do not want to sell or ship.

SEE ALSO **5.5** "How can I prevent other potential problem buyers from bidding on my items?"

SEE ALSO **6.3** "How can I stop buyers from bidding on my items if they live in a country where I do not want to ship?"

For now, look at it positively. Your item sold. Look at your buyer's feedback. Is it at least 20, and 100 percent positive? Now look at the country where your buyer resides. Is it a country such as Canada, the United Kingdom, Australia, Japan, or a country in Europe? Did the international customer pay you and is her money in your PayPal account in U.S. funds? If all the answers are "yes," then I would not be too concerned about shipping to your new international customer.

If the buyer's feedback is poor or you are still uncertain about shipping the item, consider cancelling the transaction. The reason for cancellation would be that the buyer lives in a country where you do not ship. You can then send a Second Chance Offer to the next highest bidder if you want to.

SEE ALSO **5.3** "The winning bidder has buyer's remorse and wants to cancel the transaction. What should I do?"

10.12 "How should I ship an APO or FPO package?"

A customer with an Army or Air Force Post Office (APO) or the Navy's Fleet Post Office (FPO) address just means that he is in the military stationed overseas or in U.S. territories such as Guam. I receive many of these orders and they are great customers.

Only the USPS is allowed to ship items to APO/FPO addresses. You can use the free USPS Priority Mail boxes to ship the item. The post office also has Flat Rate Priority Mail APO/FPO boxes available from their website (and in-store if you live near a military base). They offer discounted rates when you use these boxes, compared to domestic Flat Rate boxes.

You will need to complete Customs Declaration PS Form 2976-A available at your post office. The cost to ship to an APO address is the same as shipping within the 48 states (sometimes cheaper if you use the Flat Rate APO/FPO boxes).

The estimated delivery times from the USPS is only to deliver the package to a military base on either coast. Therefore, delays can occur from that point until final delivery. There is little need for concern about negative feedback from late deliveries. Military personnel are used to the delays. A helpful website that specializes in information about APO/FPO shipments is www.oconus.com/ZipCodes.asp.

One last thought on APO/FPOs. These individuals are in the Armed Services serving our country overseas. If you can throw in a freebie with their merchandise, please do. They will greatly appreciate it and it is certainly deserved.

10.13   "Can I use Calculated Rates for international shipments when creating my listing?"

Yes. You can either choose to offer a Flat Rate for each country or let eBay and the USPS provide a Calculated Rate. There is no difference in the process for creating a Calculated Rate for domestic or international addresses.

If you choose to use a Flat Rate, note that with the USPS, the rate is the same anywhere within a country. Therefore, it is easy to determine what the shipping rate will be for each major country where you ship. I suggest you include those rates in your listing's description.

Just make a list of the major countries in your description, such as Canada, the UK, Japan, and Australia. I suggest simply having one listing for Europe, as the rates to most European countries are the same.

Then visit the usps.com website to determine the rates to these countries and place them in your listing as shown below. This process will take less than two minutes and it greatly enhances your chance of receiving international bidders, as you have already answered the international shipping rate question.

Our international shipping rates for this item are as follows:

Australia	$ [insert Flat Rate here]
Canada	$
Europe	$
Japan	$
UK	$

And so on ...

SEE ALSO **9.22** **"How can I determine how much to charge for shipping?"**

10.14 "Where can I go to learn more about international shipping and Customs?"

The following websites have considerable information about international shipping:

- www.export.gov
- www.wcoomd.org
- www.export.gov/exportbasics
- www.sba.gov/aboutsba/sbaprograms/internationaltrade

eBay Stores

An eBay Store presents a more professional appearance to your buyers and provides another way for you to market your business. While not all sellers require a store, there are certain features and benefits that come from store ownership.

Opening an eBay Store

11.1 "What is an eBay Store?"

An eBay Store is much like having your own website, only it's on eBay. All of your product listings will be displayed in your store and organized in the categories you determine.

Your store comes with a search tool so buyers can quickly find specific items. When you keep your store well stocked, it encourages buyers to browse and make impulse purchases.

11.2 "Why would I need an eBay Store?"

To add a new sales channel to your eBay business. Stores are a great way to market or cross-promote add-on and accessory products. If you sell specialty or niche items that have a common theme, they can be nicely displayed in an eBay Store. If you sell items that have accessories, sell the main items in your standard listings and the accessories in your store.

You can also save money on Insertion Fees when you own a store. As a storeowner, you pay much less for Insertion Fees than you would if you listed all your items as standard listings on eBay. The Insertion Fee for a store item is also the same whether the listing has a quantity of 1 or 1,000.

SEE ALSO **11.5 "What are the store fees?"**

Store items are also available for 30 days rather than the 10-day maximum for standard Auction-Style listings. You can even set up your store items to renew every 30 days (Good 'Til Cancelled) rather than have the listings end.

11.3 "When should I open an eBay Store?"

You don't need a store if you are just getting started on eBay. It is also not necessary if you are just cleaning out your closet, basement, or garage. In fact, many successful PowerSellers don't even have an eBay Store.

Once you have found your products and designated the primary products from the accessories and secondary products, it is time to open a store. If you sell related items, such as accessories or add-ons, you need a store.

For example, if you sell jewelry, list the ring on eBay as a standard listing. Then invite the buyers to your store to purchase the matching necklace. While they are at your store, they can view all of your jewelry as well as other items such as cleaning kits.

11.4 "What are the store subscription levels?"

There are three different levels of eBay Stores:

Basic. Your first store opening should probably be at the Basic level. It is for casual and part-time sellers. The subscription includes unlimited product listings and five fully customizable catalog pages. You will have access to tools that help you create and manage special promotional e-mail campaigns for your store newsletter subscribers. The Basic level enables you to have an e-mail list of up to 5,000 subscribers.

Premium. The Premium level is for advanced or full-time sellers. Included in the subscription are all of the features in the Basic package, plus an upgrade to 10 catalog pages and 7,500 subscriber e-mails. Premium Stores also include a free subscription to Selling Manager Pro, a discount on Picture Manager, and more advanced store-traffic analysis reports.

Anchor. Anchor Stores are for professional eBay sellers with larger businesses. Included are all the features of Basic and Premium, plus 10,000 subscriber e-mails, 15 catalog pages, and a free subscription to Picture Manager.

POWERSELLER TIP

If you consider yourself a part-time seller, then start with a Basic Store. You can always upgrade to Premium at a later time. If, however, you are planning to subscribe to Selling Manager Pro and also want an eBay Store, then you should open a Premium Store and receive all the products and additional services for a discounted package price.

11.5 "What are the store fees?"

Your total store fees consist of your monthly subscription fee, as well as the Insertion Fees when listing store inventory, and the Final Value Fees when a store item sells.

Current Monthly Subscription Fees:

Basic	$15.95
Premium	$49.95
Anchor	$299.95

The Insertion and Final Value Fees change periodically. To find the current fees for eBay Stores, click the **Help** link and type **eBay Stores Fees.**

11.6 "How do I open an eBay Store?"

Go to http://stores.ebay.com, and select **Open a Store.** You can then use the Quick Store Setup tool to easily construct your store. Once your store is created, use the **Seller Manage Store** link at the bottom of your store page to set your own preferences and customizations.

11.7 "How do I determine my categories?"

Think of a large retail store. There are departments for men's, women's, and children's clothing. They also have consumer electronics, automotive, pharmacy, and food. What if there were no separate departments and all of the items were placed randomly throughout the store? That is precisely why they are called "department stores."

The categories of your eBay Store organize your products under common themes for easy browsing and shopping. Place related items in the same category. For help determining the names of categories, visit websites or other eBay Stores that sell similar items and see the names they have chosen. I always like to add a "Bargain Bin" category to an eBay Store. Place the items there that are not selling as well and have a clearance sale.

You are allowed up to 300 different categories and subcategories. You can also display up to three levels of subcategories. However, imagine if you landed on a website and you could scroll down 300 categories or subcategories. A store becomes much too cluttered in my opinion after about 25 primary categories. If you have so many products that you need that many categories, I suggest you open a new eBay account and a new store.

Store Items

11.8 "What type of items should I list in my store?"

List your best-selling, most popular products on eBay using standard auction or Fixed Price listings. Place secondary items in your store that are impulse buys for the items you sell.

For example, sell children's winter sweaters and jackets in your standard listings; then place the matching mittens, hats, and scarves in your store for add-on sales. Be sure to mention your other store items in the description of your standard listings and provide a link to your store.

11.9 "How do I create a store listing?"

When you use eBay's Sell Your Item form, you are asked what type of format you want for the listing: Auction-Style, Fixed Price, or Store Inventory. Choose Store Inventory. Note that all listings created for Store Inventory will have Buy It Now prices. All other methods for store listing creation are the same as standard eBay listings.

11.10 "Will the items in my store show up in keyword searches?"

No, not usually in standard eBay searches. If a standard search produces fewer than 30 listings, however, eBay will include some store item listings (starting with the cheapest price). See the next question.

11.11 "How do buyers find my store items?"

A buyer can choose to include store items in his searches. He may also choose to search only for Fixed Price items. This would include store items.

The most common way buyers find your store items is by you inviting them to visit your store. EBay automatically provides a link in your standard listings for this purpose. However, in my descriptions, I try to catch the eye of buyers by mentioning other items that are in my store. I then provide a clickable link to my store or even directly to a particular item.

Marketing an eBay Store

11.12 "Can I just open an eBay Store and sell items from it like a website and not list any items on eBay?"

No, I do not recommend this. Even if you have set up your eBay Store correctly to receive Internet searches from Google, Yahoo!, and other search engines, your results will be very disappointing if this is your sole marketing strategy.

SEE ALSO **11.16** *"How do I set up my store to appear on Internet search engines?"*

You really must have eBay listings running concurrently and constantly on eBay to "draw" your customers to you. You need the leverage of these listings to help browsers and buyers find you. Then within your description, list other related items that will send buyers to your eBay Store. This is very easy to accomplish using the **Click Here** hyperlinks in Turbo Lister.

SEE ALSO **5.25** *"What is Turbo Lister?"*

11.13 "How do I market my store?"

Inserting the **Click Here** hyperlinks in all of your standard listing descriptions is the best way to attract traffic to your store. Cross-promoting your store items with standard listings is another successful method.

You should also create e-mail campaigns to market to your customers. On all of your listings, a link is provided for buyers to **Sign Up to Store Newsletter.** This doesn't mean you have to create an actual newsletter. It does enable you to gather e-mail addresses of your buyers and even browsers. This is all done automatically by eBay. You can then create monthly or periodic e-mail marketing campaigns promoting new products or sale items. Use e-mail sale campaigns in conjunction with Markdown Manager to create an attractive store with several sale items.

SEE ALSO **11.19 "What is Markdown Manager?"**

You can also create and print flyers from the templates provided by eBay. The flyers will promote your eBay Store. They can be placed in packages you are shipping or given out along with your business card at trade shows.

11.14 "What is upselling or add-on selling?"

The terms are sometimes used interchangeably. Upselling is when a retailer encourages a customer to upgrade from the product she is interested in buying to a better model or unit. Add-on sales occur when you encourage the customer to buy additional items related to her main purchase such as tennis balls when buying a tennis racket, or coffee filters when buying a new coffee maker. Even the post office asks if you want stamps every time you visit their service counter.

11.15 "How does eBay cross-promote my store items with my regular listings?"

One of the benefits of store ownership is that eBay will automatically cross-promote your store items with your standard listings. EBay randomly chooses four items from your store based on the category you select when creating the standard listing. You can also manually change the items that will be displayed.

There are two levels of cross-promotion. The first level is when a buyer is browsing your standard listing. You would want to show similar items of interest. For example, if you are selling guitars, show four other makes or models.

The second level of cross-promotion occurs after a customer has won your auction, and it appears during checkout. You would then cross-promote the guitar strings, straps, cords, and stands in your store.

11.16 "How do I set up my store to appear on Internet search engines?"

This is such an important question. There are so many sellers, even PowerSellers, who have not set up their stores to maximize searches from outside of eBay.

First, the biggest mistake eBay storeowners make is that they have written their store title, description, and categories as if they are writing an advertisement. The secret to properly setting up your store is to use "keywords" just like you do in your listing's title. You should not write ad copy, but use searchable keywords that Internet buyers will use and that Internet search engines will recognize.

Therefore when a buyer on the Internet types in one of those keywords, the search engine will respond with "Want to search for this item on eBay?" When the person clicks on that link, she can land on the list of stores that have the item, possibly including yours.

Here's how to use keywords to help give you a higher placement in Internet search results:

1. Login to My eBay and view your store's page.
2. Select **Seller Manage Store** at the bottom of the page.
3. Select **Search Engine Keywords.**
4. In your Store Front Page, type the names of all the items you carry. Use brand names if you carry them. You only have up to 300 characters to work with so use them wisely.
5. Do the same for your store categories. As much as possible, use meaningful category descriptive keywords that an Internet searcher would use.

Give your title, keywords, and categories some careful thought. This is how buyers on the Internet will eventually land at your store. It will take about three months for the entire Internet spiders and crawlers to find your site when set up properly.

POWERSELLER TIP

Search engine optimization (SEO) is the most important component to your store's success. SEO experts can charge thousands of dollars to properly set up an Internet website. The best information I have found on this subject for eBay storeowners is a video series available at www.StoresSuccessVideo.com/studentrate. It shows you step-by-step how to get your store products on the first page of Google search results.

11.17 "What should I write in my About the Seller page?"

Write about your commitment to excellent customer service. The reassuring message you want to convey is that the customer will have a positive experience when dealing with you. Write about your 100 percent money-back guarantee and other policies. Look at the About the Seller pages for your top competitors or other experienced PowerSellers. When you find a few that you like, rewrite them to create a friendly, positive message about you, your business, products, and commitment to customer satisfaction.

Other eBay Store Questions

11.18 "How do I manage my store?"

There are several tools available from eBay so you can automate and manage your store. This includes vacation mode, Markdown Manager, and Store Traffic Reports. Once you have opened a store, you can manage it by setting your store preferences using the **Seller Manage Store** link. See the next two questions for more information.

11.19 "What is Markdown Manager?"

Markdown Manager is an attractive way to display sale items in your store. Using this tool, you can display an eye-catching red sales tag on items you decide to discount in your store. You can reduce the price by a percentage or by a specific dollar amount. This is a good tool to use when creating marketing campaigns.

SEE ALSO **11.13** "How do I market my store?"

11.20 "How can I track sales in my store?"

Storeowners can receive free traffic reports from eBay. These are quite comprehensive and provide valuable insights about your buyers' browsing and purchasing preferences. Depending on your store subscription level, the reports can reveal the number of buyers visiting your store, the keywords they used to find you, if your buyers originated on eBay or the Internet, and which search engine they used to find you. Learn more using the link http://pages.ebay.com/storefronts/tracking.html.

11.21 "How does eBay's Store Referral Credit program work?"

If an eBay storeowner also has a website, he can receive credit for sending customers to his eBay Store. Using eBay's Store Referral Credit Program, buyers sent from a storeowner's website are tracked to the seller's eBay Store. If the buyer purchases an item from his store, eBay will refund 75 percent of the Final Value Fee of the product purchased.

When you sign up for the Store Referral Credit program, you will receive special codes from eBay to use in the link. You must insert the correct codes and land at the correct pages in your store in order for the credit program to work. If you are sending traffic to your store but not receiving the credit, you probably have a mismatch between the code and the landing page. To learn more, select **Help** and type **about the store referral credit.**

Product Sourcing

The profitability of your eBay business depends primarily on the items you choose to sell. For many sellers on eBay, their product choices come mainly from guesswork. These sellers experience limited success, disappointing profits, and discouragement.

When I first began selling on eBay, searching for items to sell consumed the vast majority of my time. Even when I found an item I was interested in selling, I was often unsure about the supplier's reliability. Product selection and sourcing from reputable suppliers is still the major problem for eBay sellers today, but it doesn't have to be.

In this chapter I will cover the most often asked questions about product sourcing. I will also share my method for finding profitable products and reputable suppliers.

Finding Products to Sell

12.1 "What should I sell on eBay?"

This is the question I receive most often from my students and when consulting with clients. The person who asks this question wants me to provide an answer, such as "Sell toys, or automotive accessories." They want to know what is hot right now. However, they really are asking the wrong question.

EBay markets move rapidly. Even if I told you that a particular market was hot on eBay today, what will you do in six months when that market has cooled? My advice for a product choice is not what you need. What I can tell you is how and where to find ideas and products that suit your business goals.

So what should you sell? You should sell items that are profitable! While that seems like an obvious statement, the fact is that many eBay sellers are not doing this. The problem is that they have no method to their product-selection process. They run across an item of interest and "give it a shot" on eBay. Sometimes it works and sometimes it doesn't. If they make too many product-selection mistakes, it can become very costly.

You don't have to do this. In fact, you can determine if items will be profitable before you make any product purchases. The biggest difference between a typical seller on eBay and a professional is that the amateur uses guesswork for her product selection, while the professional has a methodology to determine the product's chance for success even before she purchases the item for resale. See the next question.

12.2 "What advice do you have for determining what to sell?"

You need a method that produces quality product ideas, and then enables you to determine if the products are profitable. Once you have decided what your products will be, you must then purchase them only from reputable suppliers.

Step 1: Develop Quality Ideas

Product ideas can come to you anywhere and at any time. You can hear about a product from friends, TV, or the radio, or read about it in magazines or the newspaper, or even scan the Yellow Pages. You can also scan categories on eBay looking for product ideas, or spy on eBay or Internet sellers who sell products of interest.

Whatever method you use to develop product ideas, run them through your "decision filter" to eliminate the outliers. The quality ideas that are left then need to be tested for profitability.

SEE ALSO **12.3 "Are there products I should avoid selling on eBay?"**

Step 2: Determine if the Products are Profitable

Once you have an idea for a product, determine if the item is profitable on eBay. You can use a manual method or software tools specifically developed for this purpose. If you choose to do this manually, use the research method described in question 4.34. If you would like software tools to do this quickly, use HammerTap and Instant Product Research (see question 5.26).

Step 3: Find Reputable Suppliers

Now that you've found quality products that have also passed your profitability tests, it's important to find reputable suppliers of the product.

SEE ALSO **12.23** "How can I find reputable wholesalers, liquidators, importers, and drop shippers?"

Note that I provide a complete methodology how to develop quality product ideas, determine product profitability, and find reputable suppliers in the companion to this book, *eBay Rescue Profit Maker* (Alpha Books, 2009).

12.3 "Are there products I should avoid selling on eBay?"

Yes. The following are products that I think you should *not* try to sell on eBay:

- Products that are already saturated on eBay.
- Items that sell for little to no profit.
- Oversized items that are difficult to ship.
- Items that are prohibited on eBay.
- Recalled items.

SEE ALSO **4.63** "Can I sell recalled items on eBay?"

SEE ALSO **4.64** "I see sellers who are selling prohibited items or are doing something that violates eBay rules. Why can they get away with it?"

- Items under $10 (usually just not enough profit).

- Your own handmade crafts. Unless you have a very creative idea, don't sell items that anyone else could make. There is usually little demand on eBay for these common handcrafted items.

12.4 "What is a niche market?"

There are different levels to a marketplace. On eBay, we tend to think of products in categories. Then we can drill down even further to several subcategory levels. A niche market usually resides a few subcategory levels down from a general market category on eBay.

The advantage of a niche is that there is limited competition. An ideal niche then is a subcategory market on eBay that has products with high demand and low competition. While it takes some effort to find one, you can make a lot of money in an ideal niche.

12.5 "How do I find my niche market?"

When you are conducting research for your ideas, you may find a product or group of products that are profitable but also have high demand and little competition. These are not usually found with items that have mass appeal, but with items that are more unusual or harder to find.

Hobbyist products are a good place to look. So are any products that solve or fix a problem such as replacement parts. What if you found a heavy demand for swimming pool replacement filters? That is a niche with limited appeal to the masses. If you find there is little competition on eBay and the filters that are selling are also quite profitable, then you have found an ideal niche!

12.6 "Do you recommend specializing in one niche or selling several types of products?"

Both. As you grow your eBay business, you should specialize in several niches and sell only the profitable products in each niche. You should also "general sell" products that you come across, such as liquidation items, which have nothing to do with any of your specialized niches. This is why I have several eBay accounts and stores, each selling a variety of products unrelated to my other specialty niches.

Product Suppliers

12.7 "What do you think of flea markets, and garage and estate sales, as sources of products for eBay sellers?"

They are all often-used sources of products for eBay sellers. I know many successful sellers who use them exclusively to find their products.

You may be like a family member of mine. He has developed a sense of knowing what to purchase and what to leave on the table at estate sales. He studies books and guides for collectibles and old recordings. Recently at a private sale he purchased a large record collection for $1,700. He had a starting price of $9.99 on just one 78 RPM record and it sold for $2,025.

Educate yourself so that you can recognize gems as well as junk. A friend's neighbor had three old fishing rods he was going to throw away. My friend suspected they were collectibles and said he would try to sell them on eBay. When he investigated further, he discovered they were made in France in the 1950s. The first rod sold for $173, the second for $756, and the third for $1,100.

Various sources of products are what make eBay interesting and fun. I choose my items in different ways. Personally, I do not particularly enjoy going to garage or estate sales. Almost all of my product searching is done online using my research software tools and methods.

SEE ALSO **12.23** "How can I find reputable wholesalers, liquidators, importers, and drop shippers?"

Other successful sellers anticipate and certainly enjoy estate and garage sales. If you enjoy the hunt and know what to look for, then go and have fun.

POWERSELLER TIP

Don't forget to visit local businesses as well. Many of them may be willing to let you liquidate some of their products. In particular, I am thinking of small companies located in industrial parks.

12.8 "What is a wholesaler?"

Wholesalers purchase large quantities of products from manufacturers and store them in warehouses. Most wholesalers specialize in stocking inventory for a particular industry. Retailers then purchase their products from the wholesalers in much smaller quantities and resell those products to consumers. Therefore there are three markups along the supply chain: the manufacturer's markup to the wholesaler, the wholesaler's markup to the retailer, and the retailer's markup to the consumer.

12.9 "Why don't wholesalers just sell directly to the public?"

For the same reason you don't buy your new car from the factory. This is not how the distribution supply chain works. If wholesalers sold directly to a customer, their retailers would revolt. Also, they don't want to bother selling one item at a time. They are moving hundreds or thousands of products a day depending on the industry. They need volume to make their profit margins. They want to sell to retailers, not consumers.

There are some wholesalers that will sell one product at a time for a retailer. They will even ship the product directly to the retailer's customer. They are called drop shippers.

SEE ALSO **12.15** "What is a drop shipper?"

12.10 "What is the difference between a wholesaler and a distributor?"

Distributors are usually smaller wholesalers who specialize in certain categories of an industry. They usually employ a sales staff that you can order your products from, rather than an impersonal, online order entry system. Distributor prices are usually a bit higher than larger wholesalers, but their minimum order quantities are usually less. As an eBay seller, consider them both the same for your product-sourcing needs.

12.11 "How can I find the manufacturer or wholesaler for a particular product?"

If you have the product package, find the manufacturer's name, phone number, or website printed on the package. If you've only heard about a product and do not have the package, go to Thomas Register at www.thomasnet.com to find the manufacturer. If that fails, conduct an Internet search for the product along with the keyword "manufacturer." Once you have found the manufacturer, contact them and ask who the wholesaler is for your area.

12.12 "Do I need a business license to purchase from wholesalers?"

Yes, but a business license is very easy and inexpensive to obtain. The benefits far outweigh the cost and time spent to obtain the license. Without a business license, your product sources are severely limited. A business license gives you access to a large and diverse group of product options, types, and suppliers (see Chapter 14).

12.13 "Can I purchase wholesale items on eBay?"

Yes, you can. Login to eBay and search for keywords such as lot, lots, bulk, surplus, wholesale, case, and pallet. Did you know that eBay has an entire category for buying and selling wholesale lots? Check out http://reseller.ebay.com/ns/wholesalelots.html. Once there, you will find multiple listings of wholesale lots in multiple subcategories.

Be sure that you do your research on eBay first, before you place a bid on items listed in these wholesale categories. In some cases, they are being sold in bulk because the seller can't move them individually. Do your research and make sure your item will be profitable if sold separately.

12.14 "What is eBay's Reseller Marketplace?"

If you are a PowerSeller, you are allowed to purchase items from eBay's Reseller Marketplace at www.ebay.com/reseller. This marketplace has hundreds of product suppliers that have been preapproved by eBay. They are a source of both new and refurbished products.

Most of the items here sell in lots, so you would need adequate storage space. You must also have a sufficient budget because the average lot sale is between $1,000 and $5,000.

12.15 "What is a drop shipper?"

Wholesalers, who will ship an individual item directly to a customer for a retailer, are called drop shippers. Online retailers can then list items they do not actually stock. When the item sells, they contact their drop shipper to send the item directly to the customer.

12.16 "Do you recommend using drop shippers?"

Yes, because using them provides you with budgetary leverage. With drop shipping, you are able to increase your product line because you are not spending money shelving and storing inventory for future sales. In theory, you have zero inventory cost until after your product sells.

There are also a couple of disadvantages with drop shippers. First, you are placing your Feedback Score in the hands of your drop shipper. Be sure that you are dealing with a reputable drop shipper. Second, you need to keep some inventory in your own private stock in case your drop shipper is temporarily out of stock for the item you just sold.

SEE ALSO **12.23 "How can I find reputable wholesalers, liquidators, importers, and drop shippers?"**

I also would not recommend the use of drop shipping for new eBay sellers. Wait until you have a bit of experience before you shift into this gear.

12.17 "What is a liquidator?"

Manufacturers, wholesalers, importers, and retailers use liquidation wholesalers (liquidators) to divest their unwanted inventory. It could be inventory that is seasonal, older models, closeouts, restocks, or repackaging.

The liquidators unload and resell the items for a fraction of their retail value. This is a good place for eBay sellers to look for quality products at bargain prices.

POWERSELLER TIP

I use liquidation sites quite a bit to find my products. In fact, I use www.whatdoisell.com/studentrate to find reputable liquidators. Then I scour the products that are available from these liquidators. When I find a product that looks promising, I use HammerTap and Instant Market Research to quickly determine if the products will be successful on eBay.

12.18 "What is a lot?"

Most liquidation sites require that you purchase in "lots." A lot means a group of items. When you purchase a lot from a supplier, you have to purchase the entire lot of possibly 100 or maybe even 5,000 items. They can be all the same item or several different types.

12.19 "Can I buy directly from a manufacturer?"

If the manufacturer is small, then sometimes you can purchase directly from them for resale. In most cases, however, you must purchase your products from a wholesaler, liquidator, or importer.

12.20 "What is an importer?"

An import wholesaler usually has a very narrow product line. However, they have huge inventories of that particular product line. You purchase from importers to receive a better discount off the price of wholesale products. The disadvantage is that an importer's minimum order requirement is usually much larger than a standard wholesaler's. Only use an importer if you have cornered a niche on eBay with very high demand. Otherwise you will have too much inventory.

12.21 "How can I establish accounts with Asian importers?"

A popular website to learn how to find and work with reputable importers is www.importexporthelp.com. I also discovered Global Sources www.globalsources.com during a recent "eBay Live" convention. They are a free site that can connect eBay sellers with Asian manufacturers and importers. They also offer reports that are available for purchase to explain the process for specific import markets and products.

Also check out www.alibaba.com. You can browse their site looking for manufacturers listed under various categories.

12.22 "What are middlemen?"

Look at the following chart and you can quickly see the problem. Middlemen advertise themselves as wholesalers, but in fact they are retailers selling to unsuspecting eBay and Internet sellers.

Middlemen in the Distribution Supply Chain

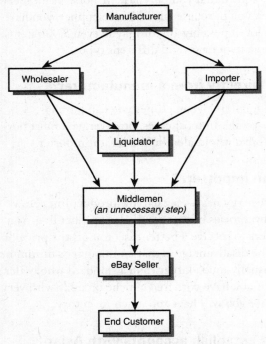

Middlemen in the Distribution Supply Chain

They constitute an unnecessary step in the distribution supply chain because you should be able to purchase from all of their sources without going "through" them. This causes the cost of their products to be unfairly inflated to the eBay seller.

How to Spot Middlemen

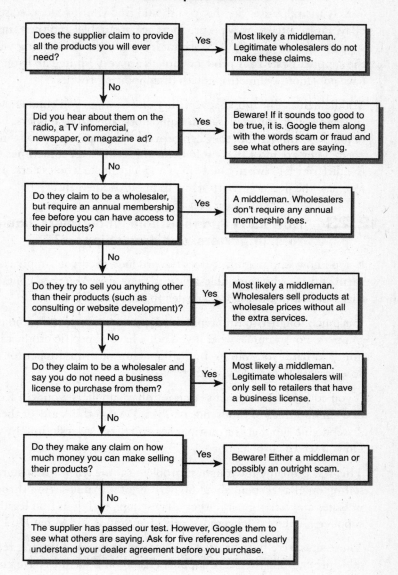

Does the supplier claim to provide all the products you will ever need?	Yes →	Most likely a middleman. Legitimate wholesalers do not make these claims.

No ↓

Did you hear about them on the radio, a TV infomercial, newspaper, or magazine ad?	Yes →	Beware! If it sounds too good to be true, it is. Google them along with the words scam or fraud and see what others are saying.

No ↓

Do they claim to be a wholesaler, but require an annual membership fee before you can have access to their products?	Yes →	A middleman. Wholesalers don't require any annual membership fees.

No ↓

Do they try to sell you anything other than their products (such as consulting or website development)?	Yes →	Most likely a middleman. Wholesalers sell products at wholesale prices without all the extra services.

No ↓

Do they claim to be a wholesaler and say you do not need a business license to purchase from them?	Yes →	Most likely a middleman. Legitimate wholesalers will only sell to retailers that have a business license.

No ↓

Do they make any claim on how much money you can make selling their products?	Yes →	Beware! Either a middleman or possibly an outright scam.

No ↓

The supplier has passed our test. However, Google them to see what others are saying. Ask for five references and clearly understand your dealer agreement before you purchase.

How to Spot Middlemen

Using middlemen, you can only sell the products they provide. This is exactly the opposite way that you should find your products to sell on eBay. First, determine what products are profitable, and then find the supplier of those products. With middlemen, you are starting with the supplier first. Your product choices are very limited and you will have enormous competition with disappointing results.

Middlemen can be found advertising online when you conduct an Internet search for wholesalers, liquidators, and drop shippers. Beware of people claiming that they can provide all the products you will need. They are most likely middlemen. It is difficult sometimes to tell the difference between middlemen and legitimate wholesalers. Therefore, use the decision chart "How to Spot Middlemen."

12.23 "How can I find reputable wholesalers, liquidators, importers, and drop shippers?"

If you know who manufacturers the product, then you simply contact them and ask who the wholesaler is in your area. You then contact that wholesaler and ask for a dealer application.

It is much tougher to find reputable liquidators, importers, and drop shippers. For example, what if you don't have a specific product in mind? What if you want to find a liquidator or drop shipper for RV accessories? Where do you start?

If you conduct an Internet search for eBay suppliers, you will see tens or even hundreds of thousands of links. Do you think any of these are disreputable suppliers or outright scam artists? Most definitely, yes! Do you see the problem here?

This was probably the toughest problem for me when I first started selling on eBay. I spent about 80 percent of my time sifting through websites and talking with other eBay sellers, trying to find legitimate suppliers. Then I discovered Worldwide Brands and What Do I Sell®.

These sites were both created to solve the problem of finding reputable product suppliers. All suppliers listed on their sites have gone through a very stringent screening process. In fact, this process will eliminate most suppliers who apply to their sites. You can then quickly find suppliers for the type of products you are interested in selling.

As a member of these two sites, you can eliminate the disreputable product supplier problem. Using their databases, you can find a variety of suppliers for the products you are interested in selling such as liquidators, wholesalers, light-bulk wholesalers, large-volume wholesalers, importers, and drop shippers. Not every product will have a supplier listed on their sites. Maybe none were approved by their screening process. However, I have found that, as a member of both sites, I have been able to find at least one type of supplier for most of the items I am interested in selling.

What Do I Sell® has a monthly membership fee, and Worldwide Brands offers a lifetime "Product Sourcing Membership" for a one-time fee. Learn more and receive a membership discount at these sites:

www.whatdoisell.com/studentrate

www.worldwidebrands.com/studentrate

Other Product Sourcing Questions

12.24 "I have some tough competition on eBay for the items I want to sell. Can I compete?"

Competition is inevitable for most items you will sell on eBay. You can certainly compete as long as there is equal demand for the product.

Are the products in question selling well and are they profitable? Use the method described in 4.34 to conduct research on the particular items you want to sell. Your research will then give you a more complete answer.

12.25 "What do you think of information products on eBay and the Internet that promise to reveal 'secret sources of products' for eBay sellers?"

Keep your money. Most of this so-called information is from middlemen, is a severely outdated supplier list, or is an outright scam. There is no secret source for eBay sellers. Find your products using the methods and sources I have provided in this chapter.

POWERSELLER TIP

Beware of "free eBay seminars" you see advertised in the newspaper, on the radio, or sometimes on TV infomercials. They entice you to come to a free eBay seminar coming to your area. Once you are there, they flip you over to purchase their ridiculously overpriced websites and associated products to sell that nobody wants. When you leave, you think "Hey, what happened to the eBay seminar?"

12.26 "I have found a cheap source for a popular item. I know it is a fad, so should I even bother to sell the item?"

Absolutely! Just don't invest in too much inventory. When the fad ends, you will be stuck with the merchandise and may have to sell each item at a loss. For now, though, sell as much as you can while the fad is hot; then take the money and run!

12.27 "Where can I store my eBay inventory?"

Most sellers start out with inventory stored in closets, bedrooms, laundry rooms, or even spilling out into hallways. Then it expands to the basement or garage, and your cars move to the driveway.

If you need more space, consider neighbors, friends, storage units, or even renting storage space from local businesses that have a loading dock. Consider drop shipping some of your items so you don't have to keep a large supply of products. You can even use fulfillment centers (including Amazon.com) to store your items and do your order fulfillment for you for certain fees.

SEE ALSO 5.9 "What metrics do you use for your eBay business?"

12.28 "Are there software tools that can help me find and determine the profitability of my products?"

Yes, and they are reviewed in question 5.26.

12.29 "Which product-analysis tools do you use or recommend?"

I personally use and recommend three critical research and product-sourcing tools for my business. They are all certified by eBay and have been discussed throughout this book. Each offers a discount when using the student-rate links here:

HammerTap: www.hammertap.com/studentrate

Instant Market Research (part of their Product Sourcing Membership): www.worldwidebrands.com/studentrate

What Do I Sell®: www.whatdoisell.com/studentrate

POWERSELLER TIP

I will show you exactly how I can quickly determine if a product will be profitable on eBay using the HammerTap and Instant Market Research tools. Go to www.trainingu4auctions.com and click **Research a Product.**

12.30 "Where can I find more information about product sourcing?"

The What Do I Sell® and Worldwide Brands websites are loaded with product-sourcing information, including how to drop ship. My other two books *eBay Business at Your Fingertips* and *eBay Rescue Profit Maker* also offer significant information about finding profitable products, product sourcing, and finding and working with suppliers.

You can find government surplus on eBay at http://pages.ebay.com/governmentsurplus/index.html.

Useful information regarding importing is also available from the following sites:

www.globalsources.com

www.importexporthelp.com

http://globaledge.msu.edu

www.busytrade.com

www.rusbiz.com

Accounting and Financials

With all the other ongoing activities for a typical eBay seller, the areas of financials, accounting, and taxes are usually only an afterthought. They are, nonetheless, equally important components to an eBay business.

Taxes

13.1 "Do I have to pay taxes on the items I sell on eBay?"

I will start and end this answer the same way—ask your CPA or tax advisor. With that said, the IRS and your state's Department of Revenue (DOR) will both officially answer, "Yes, you need to report all income." When you think about it for a moment—well, of course we have to report our eBay sales as income. I think the question comes when you just want to clear out your closet and not necessarily sell for profit.

I have spoken to DOR authorities about this and, again, their answer is that you must report all income. When I pressed them a bit about the practicality of reporting income from selling a 10-year-old item from my closet, they replied, "Well, it depends on your intent." So what exactly does that mean?

If you held a garage sale, you would most likely be selling items that are 10 or more years old and would actually be taking a loss on the items sold (assuming you actually remember what you paid). Maybe you made a few hundred dollars and were glad to finally have space in your closet, and now you are finished with your eBay selling. Your intent in this case was not a profit motive but to get rid of items. The authorities have bigger fish to catch.

Now, let's say you are a successful eBay seller who is doing pretty well making a supplemental income. In order to accomplish this, you consistently purchase items from other sources for the intent of selling them on eBay for profit. This is quite a different intent and you definitely need to report this income.

Then there is the gray area. You just inherited Auntie Arlene's estate, so you keep the sentimental items and decide to liquidate on eBay whatever is remaining. What is your intent now? Is it liquidation or profit? It's not so clear. It could even depend on the price the items sell for, or if you have already paid probate taxes on them.

So there is black, white, and gray. If you are making a profit from eBay selling, do not ignore reporting it. Remember that the official word from your state's Department of Revenue or the IRS is "You must report all income." Do not make this decision lightly. Follow the advice of a CPA or professional tax advisor.

POWERSELLER TIP

Recently, the Canadian government investigated the eBay sales records of many Canadian sellers looking for tax cheats. There are rumblings that the U.S. government may want to do something similar. In fact, PayPal must now report to the IRS all eBay sellers that receive more than 200 payments in a single year, or with annual sales exceeding $20,000.

13.2 "Do I have to collect sales tax?"

A seller needs to collect sales tax for items she sells within her state. This is true whether you have a business license or not. At the time of this writing, you do not have to collect sales tax on interstate or international sales. EBay makes this process easy.

When you are listing an item on eBay using either the Sell Your Item form or Turbo Lister, there is a page provided for setting up the tax collection process. A drop-down menu on the page will enable you to select your home state. You then enter the amount of tax percentage to collect. Every state and even every county or city can be different. Ask your tax advisor what the tax rate is for your business location (or check your state's Department of Revenue website). EBay will handle the tax collection for you from this point forward.

If your buyer does not reside within your state, the tax will not appear in the invoice during checkout. If, however, your buyer resides within your state, the percentage of tax you entered earlier will be automatically added to the invoice's subtotal. This tax will be on the product only, not on the shipping. Note that some states require tax on shipping as well. If this is your case, click the **Also charge sales tax on S&H** checkbox next to your tax rate.

When an intrastate customer pays for the item, the tax will be automatically collected for you and then deposited into your PayPal account. It is up to you to track intrastate sales tax and pay the tax you have collected to your state's Department of Revenue on a monthly, quarterly, or annual basis based on your sales volume. You can easily accomplish this with eBay's Accounting Assistant or you can download your PayPal transaction history into an Excel spreadsheet. Before you begin the process of tax collection, talk to your CPA or tax advisor to agree on the proper method.

SEE ALSO   **13.8 "What is eBay's Accounting Assistant?"**

SEE ALSO   **13.9 "I don't have QuickBooks. Can I download my PayPal records into an Excel spreadsheet?"**

13.3 "Can I also take tax deductions like any other home-based business?"

Most certainly, yes, as long as your eBay selling qualifies as a business. Again, is your intent profit? Whether you are profitable or not is not as relevant as is your intent to be a profitable business. There are many legitimate tax deductions you can take when operating an eBay business. You are entitled to these deductions and should take advantage of them.

This question requires discussion that is far beyond the scope of this book and my knowledge. Ask your CPA for specific advice about deductions. There is also an excellent website and newsletter concerning taxes for online sellers by tax authority Diane Kennedy at www.taxloopholes.com.

13.4 "What do you use as your record of sale?"

All sales records are tracked electronically for you on eBay and PayPal so you do not have to keep a paper trail. If you prefer to keep one as a backup, I suggest you use a printed PayPal packing slip as your hard-copy record of sale. Print two copies of the packing slip when you are printing the shipping label from PayPal, and file one in a folder for the current month (see Appendix A).

Determining Profit

13.5 "What is the lowest-priced item you would bother to list on eBay?"

Ideally, I would want to make at least a $10 profit on any item. The reason is the time and effort required to list, sell, pack, and ship an item for $5 is the same as an item for $100. If you do not have an eBay Store or intend to cross-promote your items, then I advise selling items that bring at least $10 in profit.

However, I do list a few items that are not only less than $10 in profit, but even sell for less than $10. Why do this? Marketing!

Some of my best customers were first attracted to my business through my low-priced listings and then they were redirected to my eBay Store. While at my store, they may have purchased more items, found something that they liked and returned later to purchase, or opted-in to my e-mail newsletter list, enabling me to market to them at another time.

Even if you are selling $1,000 computers, you should consider selling $5 computer cables. A satisfied cable buyer will keep you in mind in a few months when he or his friends are searching for a new computer. Marketing!

13.6 "What do you consider a good profit margin?"

Okay, are you ready to do some math? First, let's be sure we understand the term "margin." Many people confuse profit margin with profit markup. They are not the same.

Products with a 100 percent markup (also known as "keystone" among retailers) means that the price to charge for an item is double its cost. That is a good target, although it cannot always be achieved on eBay.

An item with a 100 percent markup, however, has a 50 percent margin. Profit margin (and not markup) is what business managers use to compare profit to price. In short, it reveals whether a product or service is not only profitable, but profitable enough to bother with. It is calculated as follows:

Profit ÷ Price = Margin

Let's look at an example and say that I am selling candles. A fragrant specialty candle costs me $5 wholesale. I double it and sell it for $10, fixed price, on eBay. I am selling it as keystone because it is a 100 percent markup above the original cost.

My profit is $5 ($10 – $5), and my selling price is $10. Therefore using the formula, Profit ÷ Price = Margin, then 5 ÷ 10 = .5 or 50 percent margin. Therefore, a 100 percent markup is a 50 percent margin.

Now that you know I am talking margin and not markup, I personally would want to achieve a minimum of 25 percent margin on my products. A 50 percent or more margin for me is a good goal for most items I sell on eBay, but my minimum would be 25 percent.

Why is it important for you to understand how to calculate margin? Because it enables you to determine if a product you are thinking of selling will be profitable enough to add to your product line.

Think of this process the way a professional eBay seller does. First, she determines the average selling price for an item on eBay and then compares that to the cost she must pay for the item from her supplier. Say your research on eBay tells you that the market is holding steady at $100 for an item you wish to sell. You now need to determine what your maximum cost can be to achieve a 25 percent margin or better. Okay, let's do some math using our formulas.

If you change the formula (Profit ÷ Price = Margin) around, you get Price × Margin = Profit, or 100 × .25 = $25 profit. But wait, you are not finished. You have just determined your minimum profit. You now need to determine your minimum cost. Price – Profit = Cost, therefore $100 – $25 = $75.

Use Profit Margin to Determine Profitability

Profit Margin

Profit Margin compares the Profit to Sales ratio.

Profit ÷ Selling Price = Profit Margin

Example:

$5 Cost
$10 Selling Price

If: SP − C = Profit
Then: $10 − $5 = **$5 Profit**

If: Profit ÷ Selling Price = PM
Then: $5 ÷ $10 = .5
Or: **50% Profit Margin**

Product Profitability Formula

Use the Profit Profitability Formula to determine if a product will meet your Minimum Margin requirement.

Step 1

Selling Price × Min. Profit Margin = Min. Profit

Example:

25% Minimum Profit Margin
$100 Average Selling Price

If: ASP × MPM = Min. Profit
Then: $100 × .25 = **$25 Min. Profit**

Step 2

If: **ASP − Min. Profit = Min. Cost**
Then: $100 − $25 = **$75 Min. Cost**

Or: **$75** is the **Minimum Cost** you can pay for the item and still meet your **Minimum Margin** requirement.

Use Profit Margin to Determine Profitability

Your maximum cost for the item, then, cannot exceed $75 to achieve your desired 25 percent margin. The bottom line is this—if your supplier can provide you this product for $75 or less, you have a deal!

POWERSELLER TIP

To help make profit margin calculations easier for you, I have provided a summary chart in this book. I also have a friend, Mark Pollack (the Excel guru), who designed a simple spreadsheet you can download for free from my website to easily perform the calculations. Go to www.trainingu4auctions.com and click the **Profit Margin Calculator** link.

You now have the formulas to determine the margin requirement minimums for your business. Note also that because of the competitive eBay marketplace, different categories or products you sell may require different margin goals. For example, I may consider much less of a profit margin for an item I am drop shipping rather than an item I have to pay for upfront, take possession of, and ship.

SEE ALSO **12.15** "What is a drop shipper?"

Financial Tools

13.7 "What software application do you use to record all your sales and expenses?"

I use QuickBooks Pro. Most CPAs and even the IRS and your state's DOR use that application. Therefore it is easy to share files. EBay and PayPal also make it easy for you to download your transactions to either an Excel spreadsheet or directly to QuickBooks (see questions 13.8 and 13.9).

Note that QuickBooks is not that easy to use for the computer novice and it is a bit expensive, so be sure to speak with your CPA before you make the purchase. I also suggest you pay your CPA to set up all QuickBooks files for your business first, before you begin your data entry. It is worth the cost and time to set it up properly from the start and avoid frustration or rework later.

13.8 "What is eBay's Accounting Assistant?"

EBay's Accounting Assistant is a data transfer tool developed and maintained by eBay's professional programming staff. With this application, you can use a "wizard" to determine how you want to download the transactions details and have them automatically loaded into QuickBooks.

You can export your entire transaction detail history every quarter so that you don't have to do any additional manipulation once it is in your QuickBooks application. Note that the Accounting Assistant is included with a subscription to an eBay Store or Selling Manager. For more details, click the **Help** link and type **accounting assistant** in the search box field.

13.9 "I don't have QuickBooks. Can I download my PayPal records into an Excel spreadsheet?"

Yes, you can, and I did this every quarter when I paid my quarterly Business and Occupation (B&O) taxes, before I began using Quick-Books Pro with the Accounting Assistant. If you are new to Excel, read an instructional book, have a friend do it, or consider attending a beginning Excel course.

Here's how to download your historical transaction details from PayPal:

1. Login to your PayPal account.

2. Select the **My Account** tab.

3. Mouse over **History** and select **Download History.**

4. Choose **Custom Date Range** and provide the dates you require. For example, for all transactions from the fourth quarter of 2009, your date range would be 10/1/09 to 12/31/09.

5. Under the **File Types for Download** drop-down menu, select **Comma Delimited—All Activity.**

6. Click **Download History.**

7. You will soon receive an e-mail with download instructions.

8. Once you receive the file, open it using Excel and choose to **Save** the file to your hard drive. Use a name that is easy to identify later, such as "PayPal Download 4Q.09." This is your master file.

9. Now save the file again as "PayPal 4Q.09 revised." This will be your working file to manipulate data sorts and enter formulas, total columns, and so on, while leaving the original master file intact.

10. Now highlight all columns in the spreadsheet and do a **data sort** on **Type**.

At this point, you have all your information downloaded and sorted by type. For sales information, separate the transactions labeled "eBay Payment received" that are under the Type column by adding a few new rows above and below those transactions.

You now have a spreadsheet that has all your sales transactions that were paid through PayPal for that quarter. Now you can easily total your sales under the Gross, Fees, and Sales Tax (your in-state sales tax that was collected) columns using Excel's AutoSum feature "Σ." If this is all confusing to you, let your tax accountant, bookkeeper, or friend who understands Excel do all this for you.

13.10 "I don't have a CPA. How can I find a good one?"

I have moved several times in my life and it has been necessary that I find another good doctor, dentist, attorney, and CPA—just to name a few. A recommendation from one of these professionals is much better than the yellow pages. Professionals tend to seek and expect the best of those in other professions.

Doctors, attorneys, bank presidents, stock brokers, and other professionals usually know who the best CPAs are in your area. You can also get free legal and accounting advice from retired CPAs and attorneys at www.score.org.

14 Legalities and Liabilities

Questions often arise among eBay sellers about business licenses, liabilities, and patents. The subject of cost is often a major consideration. There are certainly times that an attorney is required in business and in other matters. Fortunately, there are less-expensive alternatives.

Business Licenses

14.1 "Do I need a business license for my eBay business?"

You do not need a business license to sell items on eBay. Whether you should obtain a license depends on what the intent is of your eBay selling.

- Are you confident that you will sell very few items a year?
- Will most of your selling be just to remove clutter from your home?
- Are you certain that you don't have any plans to purchase your items from a wholesaler, drop shipper, or other supplier?

If you answered "yes" to these three questions, then you don't really need a business license. If you answered "no" to any of them, then you should consider getting a license.

There are many good reasons for an eBay seller to obtain a business license. The main reason is that having a business license will open an entire new world of product-sourcing opportunities. Without a business license, legitimate product suppliers will not sell to you. Sellers with certain business licenses can actually benefit from lower taxes compared to sellers without a license.

14.2 "How can I decide which type of business license to get?"

I suggest you use the following steps to help you make the right decision—and all at no charge.

Talk to your CPA (or other professional tax advisor) and say that you want to obtain a small business license to sell items on eBay part time.

SEE ALSO 13.10 "I don't have a CPA. How can I find a good one?"

Tell the CPA you anticipate that your sales may grow into a full-time business. Ask him what form of business license he recommends that you apply for—based mainly on paying the least amount of taxes while still providing you with sufficient protection. In most cases, he will recommend a Limited Liability Corporation (LLC).

As you discuss your options, you may have some further legal questions. Write them down. Then instead of paying to talk to an attorney, speak to one for free at SCORE! You can find them at www.score.org. Enter your zip code to find the phone number of a chapter near you. Then call them to set up an appointment or ask them the legal questions you have over the phone.

POWERSELLER TIP

SCORE is a great source of free information for small business owners. SCORE is staffed with retired attorneys, CPAs, and business owners dedicated to helping small businesses get started. They will answer all of your business license questions free of charge and with complete confidentiality.

14.3 "How can I get a business license, cheap?"

Once your questions are answered from the steps in 14.2, you are ready to file the paperwork to get a business license in your state. You do not need to hire an attorney for this process anymore.

If you are confident in filing the paperwork yourself, you can Google the Department of Licensing (business license department) in your state. You can file the required forms online. The only fee would be the state's license fee.

If you do not feel comfortable filing all the paperwork yourself, you can still get professional help and save a lot of time and money. Instead of paying attorney fees, use an online service called "Incorporation Service Providers" to file the LLC paperwork for you. See the next question.

14.4 "What is an Incorporation Service Provider (ISP)?"

When business owners personally prepare and file their LLC formation documents with their state, they often spend more time than originally anticipated or desired in the process of researching state requirements and fees, and obtaining, completing, and submitting the appropriate documentation. If they use an attorney, they can spend well over $1,000 on legal fees.

If you use an Incorporation Service Provider instead, you answer 10 to 15 questions online and the ISP then files all the required paperwork for your state on your behalf, acting as your agent. Note that they file incorporation paperwork only, such as LLCs. They do not file paperwork for sole proprietorships or partnerships. The process is all simple, professional, and reasonable.

Two of the more popular ISPs, BizFilings and LegalZoom, are leaders in providing incorporation and other legal services to small businesses and individuals. They are dedicated to helping entrepreneurs and small business owners understand the incorporation process and they make it much easier and affordable.

They charge a very reasonable service fee plus the state filing fees. They will then file your paperwork and pay your state's required fees on your behalf as your agent. Also, you can easily obtain additional services such as a reseller certificate.

Depending on the services you request, their typical service fee savings can be as much as 80 percent off the price an attorney would charge for the same service. You can learn more about their particular services and discounted rates at www.bizfilings.com/studentrate and www.legalzoom.com/studentrate.

14.5   "What is a resale (reseller) certificate?"

Wholesalers require a resale certificate (also known as a reseller's certificate) from retailers when setting up an account. This certificate is proof that you have been licensed by your state to resell products. By presenting this certificate, a wholesaler will not charge you tax on the items you purchase from them for resale. It is assumed that you will charge the tax when selling the items retail.

One of the questions an Incorporation Service Provider will ask you when applying for a business license is whether you want a reseller's certificate. This type of question highlights the benefits of using their services versus trying to tackle all of these details yourself.

Other Legal Questions

14.6   "What is my liability if I unknowingly sell stolen items on eBay?"

I receive this question about once a month in my eBay classes. For some time, it was very difficult for me to find an acceptable answer from any resource at eBay. So I finally spoke to my attorney. His answer centered on keeping detailed records to establish proof of purchase. The better your record-keeping, the more you are protected.

Let's use a mini-warehouse auction example. Say you attended an auction for an abandoned mini-warehouse. You won a few items during the auction, including a couple of stereos. You listed them on eBay and they sold—great! Then about two weeks later, there is a knock on your door from a county sheriff wanting to have a little chat with you. In particular, he is interested in discussing two stolen stereos you recently sold on eBay. Gulp!

After you swallow hard, you show him your logbook where you have carefully recorded all purchases from nonstandard sources. You turn to the page where you recorded all of the items you won at the auction that day. Listed are not only the two stereos, but also their serial numbers and even pictures. You also have the sales receipt from the company that conducted the auction. You make a copy of all those records for the sheriff, and he promptly heads out your door and back to the warehouse to find out who had rented the unit before you purchased the items. The heat is off.

The point is, when you purchase items from a nonstandard source, it is up to you to keep detailed records of each item purchased including where, when, and from whom. Now because I am not an attorney, I will recommend that if you make regular purchases of items from nonstandard sources to sell on eBay, please see your attorney or talk to one at www.score.org for advice on this matter.

14.7 "What is my liability if I sell an item on eBay and then the buyer somehow gets hurt using that item?"

I have received this question several times. There are too many variables. Therefore, my official answer is to talk to your attorney.

With that clear, when I asked my attorney this question, he said that it would come down to whether or not you knew the item was faulty or defective before you sold it. Let's say you sold a ladder, one of the rungs broke, and the person fell and was hurt. Did you know it was defective? How do you prove you didn't know? How can the buyer prove you did? If it was a new ladder, is it your fault or the manufacturer's fault?

Do you see all the hypothetical variables here? You really need an attorney to answer this question.

POWERSELLER TIP

If you list items that could possibly cause injury, talk to your attorney and ask what type of disclaimer you need in your descriptions or policies to list those items.

14.8 "Can I sell firearms, tobacco, alcohol, or recalled items on eBay?"

The short answer is no, no, no, and no. Other examples of prohibited or restricted sales are live animals, fireworks, credit cards, and certain foods—along with many other items. However, you can sell related items on eBay. For example, you can't sell tobacco, but you can sell tobacco-related items such as lighters, cigar cases, and humidors.

Therefore, items can be allowed, restricted, or prohibited. If you have any items you are unsure about, be sure they are allowed to be sold on eBay before you list. Check out the current eBay Prohibited and Restricted policies by selecting the **Help** link and typing **prohibited items** in the search box field.

SEE ALSO **4.62** "Can I sell anything on eBay?"

14.9 "I have an idea for a new invention. Should I pursue this, and if so, how do I get a patent?"

There is no one-size-fits-all answer. Every case is unique and may require a slightly different solution. The answer depends on the industry you are about to enter, your background, skills, and finances.

Patent attorneys are usually one of the most expensive types of legal counsel, so let me guide you to more reasonable sources of information first. If you decide you still need more details, then seek the services of a patent attorney.

A good step-by-step book on the subject is *Inventing Made Easy*, by Tom and Roger Bellavance. The book provides the steps to bring an invention to market.

The link to Inventor Resources for the U.S. Patent and Trademark Office is www.uspto.gov/web/offices/com/iip/index.htm. You can also search the Internet for books, magazines, newsletters, websites, or blogs on the subject. Beware that, mixed in with the legitimate information you will find, there will be quacks and scammers wanting your money.

I recommend the magazine *Inventors Digest*. It is full of useful information and is dedicated to helping individuals get their ideas to market. You can check their website at www.inventorsdigest.com.

You will need to file a patent in order to protect your idea. In order to save money, consider filing a provisional patent before you file a full utility patent. The provisional patent is very reasonably priced and is good for one year. This will provide you the protection early in your marketing and sales efforts so no one can steal your idea. After one year, you can evaluate how your plans are progressing and decide whether you want to let it lapse or file for a full patent. You can file provisional, utility, and design patents or conduct patent searches online for very reasonable rates at www.legalzoom.com/studentrate.

A Complete Order-Fulfillment Process

This appendix provides a complete and efficient order-fulfillment process you can use to organize your shipping procedures. The process includes the steps to ship a package from the time you are paid until the pick-up of the packages from your home. If you don't already have a fulfillment process, then start with this sample one and modify it to meet your particular needs.

This process assumes you will ship your items with the United States Postal Service. You can also modify the process slightly to ship with UPS. For all other carriers, you will need to print shipping labels and schedule a home pick-up from their website.

Before we get to the detailed steps of the process, first there is some background information you need to review and understand:

- Remember not to ship anything until payment is in your PayPal account. An e-mail from eBay telling you that your item has sold is great, but wait for the second e-mail telling you that payment has been made before you begin the fulfillment process.

- I suggest you create a thank-you letter for your customers. You will place one of these letters along with a packing slip in every package you ship. The letter should be generic rather than product-specific, so it can be used for any product you sell. I suggest you take your letter to a copy center and make multiple copies. Then keep them handy in your shipping area.

- Review how to pack different types of items properly (see Chapter 9).

- Review how to print shipping labels (pre-paid postage) and schedule a home pick-up from the USPS.

A Complete Order Fulfillment Process

Phase I
ID Payments
Print Packing Slip
Print Shipping Label

Identify payment e-mails (or checks). Jot down the last 4 digits of the item number.

Go to My eBay, click the Sold page, and identify the item number. Select "Print Shipping Label" and login to your PayPal account.

Choose carrier, type, mailing date, size and weight of package, and any optional services.

Review summary page, approve payment, print shipping label and packing slip. Continue this process for all sold items. Place shipping labels and packing slips in an inbox in shipping area.

Phase II
Pack Item

Gather the item(s) sold and all packing materials.

Pack item(s) carefully, place packing slip and thank-you letter on top, then seal box.

Cut the shipping label receipt area off and file it. Attach the shipping label on the box with clear packing tape. Continue process for all packages.

Phase III
Schedule Pickup
Leave Feedback

Drop off the packages at the post office or schedule a carrier pickup.

Go to your My eBay, click the "Feedback" link, and leave positive feedback for all paying customers.

Complete Order-Fulfillment Process

In addition to the background information you will need to review, here are some tips:

- It is best if you can dedicate space in your home as your shipping area. At a minimum, you will need a sturdy table and space for boxes, packing materials, and supplies. If your floor plan allows for a room or area near your front door, that's best, because you will most likely be receiving and sending shipments through your front door. If possible, don't have your shipping area upstairs or downstairs unless you want a lot of exercise.

- Try to do all of your packing at only one time each day, or every other day. To be efficient, treat the process like an assembly line. Remain focused during this time and allow no outside distractions such as answering e-mails or the phone. To help pass time, listen to your favorite music as you pack.

Phase I. Identifying Customer Payments, Printing the Packing Slips, and Printing the Shipping Labels (Prepaid Postage)

1. Login to your e-mail account each day and scroll through the subject lines looking for e-mails that announce you have received a payment. Usually the subject line will include an Item Number and contain the words "Notification of instant payment." When you see that a customer has paid you, it is time to take action.

POWERSELLER TIP

I set up my Outlook Express to highlight the subject line of payment notification e-mails in green so they are much easier to spot.

2. Jot down the last four digits of the item number provided in the subject line of each payment notification e-mail. I also suggest you open the e-mail to quickly check that the amount paid was correct and to review other details.

3. Login to your eBay account, select **My eBay,** and view the **Sold** page.

4. Match the item number from the e-mail with the item number in the Buyer E-Mail/ID column.

5. Double-check that a PayPal payment was indeed made from this customer by observing the icon indicators at the far right of the row. The dollar-sign indicator must be solid (rather than faint).

POWERSELLER TIP

When you pay for the shipping label using PayPal, the shipping status icon on your My eBay Sold page will be bold (rather than faint). This is a great way to see at a glance any items that were paid for (the bold dollar sign) but that you have not yet shipped (a faint shipping box). This double-check ensures you have not overlooked a sale.

6. Select the **Print Shipping Label** link under the **Action** column. You will then be redirected to your PayPal account where you need to login.

7. After login, you are redirected to a page with sales and shipping information. Under **Shipment Information,** choose your carrier (USPS or UPS), service type, and enter the package size and weight.

POWERSELLER TIP

If you have multiple shipping labels to print (different customers), choose the **Create multiple labels for this order** link after you create the first label.

8. Under **Shipment Options,** enter the mailing date and any optional service you require. Note that if you are going to schedule home pick-up, choose the next day as the shipping date. Click the **Continue** button.

9. Review the summary page carefully to ensure everything is correct including the shipping rate. Edit any mistakes or click the **Pay and Continue** button.

10. A pop-up window will open. If this is your first time printing a label using this method, print a sample label first to ensure your computer and printer will print a label correctly. If the test printed correctly, choose the **Print label** button. Wait for the label to print, and then choose the **OK** button to close the print window.

11. After the shipping label has printed, choose to also print a packing slip (print two copies if you want to keep one as a hard-copy record of sale).

12. Continue this process for all the items that were paid for with PayPal or a check that has cleared. Print a shipping label and packing slip for each sale.

13. Collate each shipping label with its matching packing slip and place them in an inbox in your shipping room.

POWERSELLER TIP

When you print the shipping label, eBay will e-mail your customer stating that you have created the shipping label for the item. Many customers then assume you have shipped the product—when all you did was print the label. Therefore, either don't print the labels a few days in advance (don't print on Friday for a Monday pick-up), or send a follow-up e-mail informing the buyer that you just created a label and when her item will actually be shipped.

Phase II. Packing the Item

14. When it is time to pack, take the first packing slip and matching shipping label from your inbox.

15. Assemble the item(s) sold listed on the packing slip, the appropriately sized USPS Priority Mail box or your own box or padded envelope, and all appropriate packing materials.

16. Place the item in the box and pack it.

17. Before you close the box, place the packing slip and a thank-you letter on the very top so it is the first thing your customer will see when he opens the package. Seal the box with approved packing tape.

18. Cut off the Online Label Record (receipt) area from the shipping label. File the receipt in a shipping folder you have labeled for the current month.

19. Place the shipping label on top of the box and secure it with clear packing tape. Be careful that the tape is applied smoothly so no creases will interfere with the tracking bar code.

20. Continue this process until all packages are ready for shipment.

Phase III. Scheduling Home Pick-Up and Leaving Feedback

21. You can now either take the packages to the post office or schedule a carrier pick-up.

22. If you choose to go to the post office, there is no need to wait in line. You can walk right up to the counter and drop them off. If you have several packages and visit the post office several times a week, they may ask you to bring the packages to the back loading dock. Alternatively, many post offices now have drop-off bins in their lobbies for packages with pre-paid postage.

23. If you choose home pick-up, you must have at least one package that is Priority Mail. There is no charge for home pick-up. This is a huge benefit over all other carriers.

    To schedule home pick-up, you can choose the link to do this directly from your PayPal account. Select the **Choose multiple labels for this order** link, and then choose the link to schedule a pick-up.

    Otherwise, go to www.usps.com and select the **Schedule a Pickup** link, then choose **Carrier Pickup.** Note that you must have set up a USPS account first in order to schedule a pick-up. It is very simple to complete and there is no charge to set up the account.

24. The final step in the process is to leave positive feedback for your customer(s). In your My eBay page under **My Account,** click the **Feedback** link. Follow the steps for leaving feedback.

Resources

This appendix includes my recommended resources and helpful sites or links for eBay sellers. They are grouped alphabetically by category. Note that a link such as eBay>site map means to go to eBay's homepage and select the **Site Map** link. A link such as eBay>help>type: stores means to select the **Help** link and then type **stores** in the search box.

Antique Sites

Use these sites when conducting research on antiques:

- www.goantiques.com
- www.tias.com
- www.priceminer.com

Business License

Incorporation service providers:

- www.legalzoom.com/studentrate
- . www.bizfilings.com/studentrate

eBay

eBay help:

- eBay>help
- eBay>site map
- eBay>live help
- For PowerSellers and eBay storeowners only, phone support: eBay>help>contact us

eBay Fees:

- eBay>help>ebay.com fees
- Quick estimate calculator: www.ebcalc.com

eBay Disputes:

- My eBay>dispute console

eBay Stores:

- www.ebay.com/stores
- Videos on how to set up your store properly:
  www.storessuccessvideo.com/studentrate

Keyword Finding Tools

- http://pulse.ebay.com
- http://keyword.ebay.com
- https://adwords.google.com/select/KeywordToolExternal
- Yahoo! keyword finder: http://tinyurl.com/58y7c5
- www.wordtracker.com
- www.typobid.com or www.fatfinger.com (finds commonly misspelled keywords)

PayPal

PayPal help:

- Live PayPal representative phone support for Premier and Business levels only: 1-888-221-1161. Other members call 402-935-2050.

Photography

Photography research and reviews:

- www.cnet.com
- www.dpreview.com
- www.calumetphoto.com
- www.photoflex.com

Cloud Dome, Infinity Boards, Cubes:

- www.trainingu4auctions.com
- www.trainingu4auctions.net (eBay Store)

Product Sourcing

eBay product sourcing, trending, and analysis:

- www.whatdoisell.com/studentrate

Find reputable wholesalers and liquidators:

- www.worldwidebrands.com/studentrate (Product Sourcing Membership)
- www.whatdoisell.com/studentrate

Find reputable drop shippers:

- www.worldwidebrands.com/studentrate (Product Sourcing Membership)

Find a manufacturer:

- www.thomasnet.com

Purchase wholesale on eBay:

- www.ebay.com/reseller (for PowerSellers only)
- http://reseller.ebay.com/ns/wholesalelots.html

Government surplus on eBay:

- http://pages.ebay.com/governmentsurplus/index.html

Find importers:

- www.globalsources.com
- www.worldwidebrands.com/studentrate (Product Sourcing Membership)

Importing research:

- www.globalsources.com
- www.importexporthelp.com

- http://globaledge.msu.edu
- www.busytrade.com
- www.rusbiz.com

Shipping

Free USPS/eBay co-branded Priority Mail boxes:

- http://ebaysupplies.usps.com

Corrugated boxes:

- www.uline.com

Packing supplies:

- www.uline.com
- www.papermart.com
- www.fast-pack.com
- www.ebay.com

Large item and freight carriers:

- www.freightquote.com
- www.uship.com
- UPS Freight Service: 1-800-333-7400

APO/FPO (Military) shipping information:

- www.oconus.com/ZipCodes.asp

UltraShip postal scales:

- www.trainingu4auctions.com
- www.trainingu4auctions.net (eBay Store)

International shipping restrictions:

- http://pe.usps.gov/text/imm/immctry.htm

Software Tools

Product analysis for eBay research:

- www.hammertap.com/studentrate

Niche and product analysis for Internet research:

- www.worldwidebrands.com/studentrate (Instant Market Research, Demand, and Competition Research; all part of WWB's Product Sourcing Membership)

eBay auction-management tools:

- eBay>site map>Turbo Lister
- eBay>site map>Blackthorne
- eBay>site map>Accounting Assistant
- eBay>site map>Sales Reports
- eBay>site map>Selling Manager

Third-party auction management tools:

- Auction Hawk: www.auctionhawk.com (web)
- Auction Sage: www.auctionsagesoftware.com (desktop)
- Auction Wizard 2000: www.auctionwizard2000.com (desktop)
- ChannelAdvisor: www.channeladvisor.com (web)
- DEK Auction Manager: www.dekauctionmanager.com (desktop)
- Infopia: www.infopia.com (web)
- Marketworks (owned by ChannelAdvisor): www.channeladvisor.com/mw (web)
- Spoonfeeder: www.spoonfeeder.com (web)
- Vendio: www.vendio.com (web)
- Zoovy: www.zoovy.com (web)

Other Helpful Sites and Products

eBay Seller Evaluation Checklist:

- www.trainingu4auctions.com

Escrow service:

- www.escrow.com

Insert interactive video in your eBay listings (very cool!):

- www.deal4it.com/studentrate

Inventions:

- www.legalzoom.com/studentrate (file patent)
- www.inventorsdigest.com
- www.alibaba.com (find manufacturers)

Scams on eBay:

- www.millersmiles.co.uk/search/eBay
- Report spoof e-mails: spoof@ebay.com

Tax help for eBay sellers:

- www.taxloopholes.com

Trade shows:

- www.tsnn.com (domestic)
- http://tradeshow.globalsources.com (international)

U.S. Consumer Product Safety Commission (lists recalled products):

- www.cpsc.gov/cpscpub/prerel/prerel.html

Author's website and eBay Store for his students and readers (provides eBay buyer and seller tips, strategies, newsletter, postal scales, and photography equipment):

- www.trainingu4auctions.com
- www.trainingu4auctions.net (eBay Store)

Other eBay books by this author:

- *eBay Rescue Profit Maker* (companion to the Problem Solver) (Alpha Books, 2009)
- *eBay Business at Your Fingertips* (Alpha Books, 2008)

Index

A

abbreviations, titles, 58-59
About Me page, My World page, compared, 115-116
About the Seller page, eBay Stores, writing, 178
accounting, 197-205
Accounting Assistant, 203
accounts
  e-mail addresses, 5
  logins, 3-4
  multiple accounts, 7-8
  passwords, 3-5
  payment information, changing, 5
  PayPal, 11-20
  registration, 1-3
  suspended, 8-10
  upgrading, 7
  User IDs, 5-7
acronyms, in listings, 58
add-on selling, 176
alcohol, selling, 211
Anchor level (eBay Stores), 173
Announcement Boards (Seller Central), 83
answering e-mail, 76
APO (Army/Air Force Post Office) shipping, 168-169
Approval Tests, sellers, 31-34
artwork, 116, 128-129
Asian importers, 189
Auction-Style listings, 59-61
Auction-Style with Buy It Now listings, 60-62
Auction-Style with Reserve and Buy It Now listings, 60
Auction-Style with Reserve listings, 60-61
auctions, 38-41, 75-76
audio clips, listings, 99-100
authentic items
  confirming, 41
  selling, 111-112
automobiles, selling, 77-78

B

backdrops, photographs, 124
backgrounds, listings, 53
Basic level (eBay Stores), 172
Baydar, 76-77
Best Offer listings, 24, 60
bidders
  contacting, 22
  highest bidders, discovering, 82
  international bidders, 106-109, 168
  multiple highest bidders, 27
  nonpaying bidders, handling, 87-90
bidding, 28-30, 37-44
BIN (Buy It Now), 23
blocking
  international bidders, 106-107
  international buyers, 168
  nonpaying buyers, 89-90
bogus e-mail messages, 9-11
bold type, listings, 50
books, shipping, 149-150
borders, listings, 50
boxes, shipping, 144-148
broken items, recourse, 42
Bronze PowerSellers, 94
Business Accounts, PayPal, 12-13
business licenses
  obtaining, 207-209
  wholesalers, 187
business websites, linking, 96-97
businesses
  accounting, 197-205
  failures, 121

ISPs (Incorporation Service Providers), 209
jobs, quitting, 120-121
My eBay page, 115
products, 181-195
profitability, 117-119, 181
stores, 171-179
successful businesses, 122
vacations, taking, 113-114
Buyer Protection Policy (PayPal), 17-18
buyers
  feedback, leaving, 22
  international buyers, 106-109, 168
  negative feedback, leaving, 64
  nonpaying buyers, handling, 87-90

C

calculations
  profit margins, 200-203
  sell-through percentage rates, 91
  shipping rates, 157-158
cameras, 123-124
canceling, 75-76, 88
cancelled listings, 101
carriers
  domestic shipping, 135-143
  insurance, purchasing, 143
  international shipping, USPS, 16, 165
cars, selling, 77-78
cashier's checks, purchases, 35-36
categories, 69, 173-174
Category Tips (Seller Central), 83
CDs, shipping, 150
charging
  handling fees, 158
  sales taxes, 100-101
checking account numbers, 4
checking numbers, changing, 5
checks, 35-36, 109
claims, shipping, filing, 155
classes, eBay classes, 46
classified ad listings, 60
classified ads, posting, 97

clear glassware, photographing, 130
clothing, photographing, 129-130
Cloud Cubes (photography), 126
Cloud Domes (photography), 127
cocoons (photography), 126
collectibles, confirming authenticity, 41
collecting, sales taxes, 198-199
colored backgrounds, listings, 53
communications, international selling, 107-108
community (eBay), 83-84
competition, suppliers, 193
confirming PayPal accounts, 13-14, 17
conversion rates, sell-through percentage rates, compared, 91
copying photographs, 134
corrugated boxes, shipping, 144-147
counters, hiding, 52-53
CPAs (certified public accountants), hiring, 205
crafts, selling, 116
cross-promotions, stores, 176-177
cubes (photography), 126
customers, nonpaying customers, handling, 87-90
Customs forms, international shipping, 165-167

D

dangerous items, liabilities, 211
decision chart, domestic shipping carriers, 136
deductions (taxes), collecting, 199
defective items, recourse, 42
delivery problems, resolving, 152-155
descriptions, 46-49
DHL, 139-143
diffusers (photography), 125
discounts
  international shipping, USPS, 165
  shipping, offering, 161
Discussion Boards (Seller Central), 83
distributors, 186, 190-192
diversity, products, 184

domestic shipping, 135
  books, 149-150
  carriers, 135-140
  CDs, 150
  claims, filing, 155
  corrugated boxes, 144-147
  delivery problems, resolving, 152-155
  discounts, offering, 161
  eBay/USPS Priority Mail boxes, 144
  excessive shipping rates, 160
  handling fees, charging, 158
  home pick-ups, 141-142
  insurance, 143
  large items, 150-151
  multiple items to one buyer, 161
  packing materials, 144-148
  packing slips, 162
  padded envelopes, 144-145
  Parcel Post, 140
  postal scales, 159-160
  pre-paid postage, 141-142
  Priority Mail, 140
  rates, determining, 156-158
  tracking, 142-143
downloading
  business records, PayPal, 204-205
  photographs, 132
drop shippers, 188, 192
DSI Insurance, 151
DSRs (Detailed Seller Ratings), 32, 50
durations
  listings, 70
  Second Chance Offers, 98-99
  shipping, 79
Dutch (Multiple Item) Auction
  listings, 60, 114-115
duties, international shipping, 165-167

E

e-mail
  addresses, changing, 5
  answering, 76
  spoof e-mail messages, 9-11
earning interest, PayPal accounts, 14-15

eBay
  checking account numbers, 4
  registration, 1-3
  research, conducting, 64-69
  routing numbers, supplying, 4
eBay Marketplace Research, 44
eBay Pulse (Seller Central), 83
eBay Stores, 24
eBay Toolbar, 103
eBay/USPS Priority Mail boxes,
  obtaining, 144
eChecks, 19, 36
editing listings, 46, 73-74
EE (eBay Express!), 25
emotional bidding, avoiding, 39-40
employment, quitting, 120-121
eSnipe, 39
estate items, selling, 78
estate sales, product sources, 185
excessive shipping rates, reporting, 160
expenses, 92-93
Express Mail International® (EMI), 163

F

FCMI (First-Class Mail® International), 164
FDIC insurance, PayPal, 20
Featured Plus!, 50
FedEx, 138-143
feedback
  leaving, 22
  negative feedback, 64, 111
  positive feedback, 46
  receiving, 46, 63-64
  User IDs, changing, 5
Feedback Profiles, viewing, 22
fees
  Final Value Fees, 74
  handling fees, charging, 158
  Insertion Fees, 74
  Listing Upgrade Fees, 74
  PayPal accounts, 16
  sellers, 74-75
  stores, 173

filing shipping claims, 155
Final Value Fees, 74
financial tools, software, 203-205
firearms, selling, 211
First-Class Mail® International
(FCMI), 164
Fixed Price listings, 49, 59-62
flaws, describing, 47
flow chart, registration process, 1-3
formats, photographs, 132
formulas
profit margins, 200-203
sell-through percentage rates, 91
shipping rates, 157-158
FPO (Fleet Post Office) shipping,
168-169
fraud, avoiding, 105-107
freight, shipping, 150-151

G-H

Gallery Featured listings, 50
Gallery Pictures listings, 50
garage sales, product sources, 185
genuine items, selling, 111-112
glassware, clear glassware,
photographing, 130
GlobalEdge, 195
Gold PowerSellers, 94
guns, selling, 211

HammerTap, 44, 102, 195
handling fees, charging, 52, 158
handmade items, selling, 116
heirlooms, selling, 78
highest bidders, 82
highlights, in listings, 50
hiring CPAs (certified public
accountants), 205
hit counters, 52-53
home pick-ups, international shipping,
165
HTML (HyperText Markup
Language), Sell Your Item form, 100

I

ID Verify, 6-7
IDs (user), 5-7
importers, 189-192
ImportExportHelp.com, 195
IMR (Instant Market Research), 102,
195
In Demand (Seller Central), 83
income taxes, paying, 197-198
Indonesia, fraudulent buyers, 106
inflated shipping rates, 30
information products, 193-194
inherited items, selling, 78
Insertion Fees, 74
insurance
international shipping, 164
purchasing, 35
shipping, 143, 151
interest, PayPal accounts, 14-15
international buyers, blocking, 168
international listings, 50
international sellers, investigating, 34
international selling, 105-110
international shipping, 163-170
International Site Visibility upgrades,
110
inventions, liabilities, 212
Inventor Resources for the U.S. Patent
and Trademark Office, 212
inventories
storing, 194
turnover, managing, 93
ISPs (Incorporation Service
Providers), 209
Item Specifics, listings, 54

J-K

jewelry, photographing, 130-131
jobs, quitting, 120-121

keyword searches, 25-27
keywords, listings, 56, 58
knock-offs, selling, 70

L

languages, international selling, 107-108
large items, 131, 150-151
leaving feedback, 22
levels
    PowerSellers, 94-95
    stores, 172-173
liabilities, 210-211
licenses, 187, 207-210
light diffusers, 125
lighting, photographs, 124-125
linking websites, listings, 96-97
liquidators, 188-189, 192
Listing Upgrade Fees, 74
listings, 46
    Auction-Style, 59-61
    Auction-Style with Buy It Now, 60-62
    Auction-Style with Reserve and Buy It Now, 60
    Auction-Style with Reserve, 60-61
    audio clips, 99-100
    automobiles, 77-78
    Best Offer, 24, 60
    BIN (Buy It Now), 23-24
    bold type, 50
    borders, 50
    canceling, 75-76
    cancelled, 101
    categories, multiple categories, 69
    choosing, 60-62
    classified ad, 60, 97
    colored backgrounds, 53
    creating, 49-56
    cross-promotions, 176-177
    descriptions, 46-49
    DSRs (Detailed Seller Ratings), maintaining, 50
    durations, 70
    editing, 46, 73-74
    estate items, 78
    Featured Plus!, 50
    feedback, 63-64
    Fixed Price, 49, 59-62
    Gallery Featured, 50
    Gallery Pictures, 50
    handling fees, 52
    highlights, 50
    hit counters, 52-53
    inherited items, 78
    international exposure, 50
    international shipping rates, posting, 169-170
    International Site Visibility upgrade, 110
    Item Specifics, 54
    keywords, 56-58
    knock-offs, 70
    Multiple Item (Dutch) Auctions, 60, 114-115
    Multiple Item Fixed Price, 60
    negative feedback, 111
    photographs, 54-55, 123-134
    positive feedback, 46
    pre-filled information, 53-54
    Private Auction, 59-62
    prohibited items, 79-80
    quantities, 72-73
    recalled items, 80
    relisting, 55-56
    research, 64-69
    reserve prices, 23-24
    restricted items, 79-80
    scheduling, 70-72
    Second Chance Offers, 98-99
    Square Trade logo, 33
    Store Inventory, 59
    stores, creating, 174-175
    subtitles, 52
    successful, 84-86
    TAs (Trading Assistants), 78-79
    templates, 53
    Ten-Day, 50
    titles, 56-59
    Turbo Lister, 101

unsold items, 80-82
upgrading, 50-51
video clips, 99-100
websites, linking, 96-97
local businesses, product sources, 185
logins, choosing, 3-4
losing auctions, 38-39
lots, 189

M

M-Bags, 164
managing stores, 178-179
manufacturer photographs, copying, 134
manufacturers, purchasing directly, 187-189
Markdown Manager, 178
marketing stores, 175-178
Marketplace Research, 44
Media Mail (USPS), 149
metrics, 91-93
Microsoft Word, 48
middlemen, 190-192
misspelled words
keyword searches, 27
titles, 57-58
moiré patterns, 129-130, 133
money orders, 35-36
MoneyGram, accepting, 109
multiple accounts, 7-8
multiple category listings, 69
Multiple Item (Dutch) Auctions, 60, 114-115
Multiple Item Fixed Price listings, 60
multiple items to one buyer, 161
multiple photograph listings, 132
music, selling, 116
My eBay page, 115
My World page, 115-116

N-O

negative feedback
buyers leaving, 64

receiving, 111
User IDs, changing, 6
Newsletters (Seller Central), 83
niche markets, 184
Nigeria, fraudulent buyers, 106
non-eBay purchases, 19
nonpaying bidders, 87-90
Notepad, 48

opening stores, 172-173
order fulfillments, 46
organizing photographs, 132
outbid notices, 29-30
overbidding, 39-40

P

packing materials, 144-148
packing slips, 162
padded envelopes, 144-145
Parcel Post domestic shipping, 140
passwords, 3-5
payment information, changing, 5
payments
expensive items, 100
international selling, 108-109
PayPal accounts, 15
taxes, 197-198
PayPal
accounts, 11-20
Business Accounts, 12-13
business records, 204-205
Buyer Protection Policy, 17-18
checking account numbers, 4
fees, 16
international selling, 108
Personal Accounts, 12-13
Premier Accounts, 12
registration, 1-3
routing numbers, 4
security issues, 17
Seller Protection Policy, 18-19
Personal PayPal Accounts, 12-13
personal website linking, 96-97

phishing e-mail messages, 9-11
photographs, 54-55, 123-134
plagiarizing descriptions, 49
Platinum PowerSellers, 94
positive feedback, 46, 63-64
pre-paid postage, 141-142
postal scales, 45, 157-160
posting classified ads, 97
PowerBuyers, 43
PowerSellers, 33, 94-95
pre-filled information listings, 53-54
preferences, setting, 97-98
Premier PayPal Accounts, 12
Premium level (eBay Stores), 172
Priority Mail® domestic shipping, 140
Priority Mail® International (PMI), 164
Private Auction listings, 59-62
product-analysis software, 102-103
    HammerTap, 102
    IMR (Instant Market Research), 102
product-analysis tools, 195
products
    artwork, 128-129
    authentic products, 111-112
    automobiles, 77-78
    broken products, 42
    choosing, 181-184
    clothing, 129-130
    collectibles, 41
    costs, 93
    defective products, 42
    descriptions, 46-49
    diversity, 184
    estate items, 78
    glassware, 130
    handmade products, 116
    information products, 193-194
    inherited items, 78
    inventories, 194
    inventory turnover, 93
    investigating, 44
    jewelry, 130-131
    large products, 131
    liabilities, 210-212

Multiple Item (Dutch) Auctions,
    114-115
niche markets, 184
product-analysis software, 102-103,
    195
profitability, determining, 200-203
prohibited products, 79-80, 211
    international sales, 109-110
recalled products, 80
relisting, 55-56
research, 64-69
restricted products, 79-80
sales taxes, 100-101
shipping, 135-150, 152-160
stores, 173-178
suppliers, 185-195
TAs (Trading Assistants), 78-79
trade shows, 100
unprofitable products, 183-184
unshipped products, 42
unsold products, 80-82
profitability, 117-119, 181
    determining, 182, 200-203
prohibited items, 211
    international sales, 109-110
    selling, 79-80
purchases, PayPal accounts, 15-20

Q-R

quantities, 72-73
questioning sellers, 21
QuickBooks Pro, 203-205

rates (shipping), determining, 156-158
reactivating suspended accounts, 8-10
recalled items, 80, 211
recording sales, 200
REDOL (Registered eBay Drop-Off
    Locations), 79
Referral Credit Program, 179
reflectors (photography), 125
Registered eBay Drop-Off Locations
    (REDOL), 79

registrations, eBay and PayPal, 1-3
relisting items, 55-56
reporting, 88-89, 160
resale certificates, 210
research
  conducting, 64-69
  international sales, 110
  sellers, 30-34
  software, 102-103
Reseller Marketplace, 187
reserve prices, 23-24, 62
restricted items, 79-80
retracting bids, 28-29
return policies stating, 48-49
Romanian fraudulent buyers, 106
routing numbers, 4-5

S

sales
  dips, 116
  recording, 200
  stores, 179
sales reports, 92
Sales Reports Plus, 92
sales taxes
  charging, 100-101
  collecting, 198-199
scanning photographs, 133
scheduling
  home pick-ups, 141-142
  listings, 70-72
SCOs (Second Chance Offers), 43-44
search engine optimization (SEO), 178
search engines, eBay Stores, presence,
  177-178
searches, keyword searches, 25-27
Second Chance Offers, durations,
  98-99
Sell Your Item forms, HyperText
  Markup Language (HTML), 100
sell-through percentage rates,
  compared, 91
Seller Central, 83-84

seller photographs, 134
Seller Protection Policy (PayPal), 18-19
sellers
  Approval Tests, 31-34
  asking questions, 21
  Baydar, 76-77
  descriptions plagiarized, 49
  DSRs (Detailed Seller Ratings), 32
  failures, 121
  feedback, 22
  fees, 74-75
  international sellers, 34
  multiple accounts, 7-8
  PowerSellers, 33, 94-95
  preferences, 97-98
  purchasing options, 35
  reactivating suspended accounts,
    8-10
  researching, 30-34
  Seller Central, 83-84
  shill bidding, 40-41
  Square Trade logo, 33
  successful sellers, 122
  UPIs (Unpaid Item Disputes), 34
selling, 45, 92
  authentic items, 111-112
  automobiles, 77-78
  eBay Stores, 24
  EE (eBay Express!), 25
  estate items, 78
  expenses, 92-93
  inherited items, 78
  international selling, 105-110
  nonpaying bidders, 87-90
  order fulfillments, 46
  progress, 46
  prohibited items, 79-80
  recalled items, 80
  reserve prices, 23-24
  restricted items, 79-80
  sales reports, 92
  sales taxes, 100-101
  sell-through percentage rates, 91

stores, 171-179
TAs (Trading Assistants), 78-79
unsold items, 80-82
search engine optimization (SEO), 178
setups (photography), 126-127
shill bidding, 40-41
shipping, 46, 135
books, 149-150
carriers, 135-140
CDs, 150
claims, 155
corrugated boxes, 144-147
delivery problems, 152-155
discounts, 161
durations, 79
eBay/USPS Priority Mail boxes, 144
excessive shipping rates, 160
handling fees, 158
home pick-ups, 141-142
insurance
purchasing, 143
tracking, 35
international shipping, 108, 163
large items, 150-151
multiple items to one buyer, 161
packing materials, 144-148
packing slips, 162
padded envelopes, 144-145
Parcel Post, 140
postal scales, 159-160
purchasing, 45
pre-paid postage, 141-142
Priority Mail, 140
rates, 156-158
tracking, 142-143
purchasing, 35
Shipping Calculator, 158
shipping rates, 30, 52
Silver PowerSellers, 94
sizes of photographs, 132
small jewelry, 130-131
sniping, 38-39

software
eBay Toolbar, 103
financial tools, 203-205
product-analysis, 102-103, 195
Turbo Lister, 101
sound clips, 99-100
spamming keywords, 58
special characters keywords, 25-26
spoof e-mail messages, 9-11
spousal accounts, 8, 12
Square Trade, 33
stolen items, 210-211
Store Inventory listings, 59
stores, 171
About the Seller page, 178
add-on selling, 176
benefits, 171-172
categories, 173-174
cross-promotions, 176-177
failures, 121
fees, 173
items, 174, 181-195
jobs, quitting, 120-121
levels, 172-173
listings, creating, 174-175
managing, 178-179
Markdown Manager, 178
marketing, 175-178
My eBay page, 115
opening, 172-173
profitability, 117-119, 181
Referral Credit Program, 179
sales tracking, 179
search engines, 177-178
successful, 122
upselling, 176
vacations, 113-114
website linking, 96-97
storing inventory, 194
Styrofoam peanuts, 148
subtitles in listings, 52
suppliers of products, 185-195
suspended accounts, 8-10

T

TAs (Trading Assistants)
  becoming, 95-96
  employing, 78-79
taxes, 100-101, 197-199
templates for listings, 53
Ten-Day listings, 50
tents (photography), 126
Terapeak, 44
thumbnail pictures, 50
times for bidding, 37-38
Titanium PowerSellers, 94
titles of listings, 56-59
tobacco selling, 211
Toolbar (eBay), 103
tracking
  expenses, 92-93
  international shipping, 165
  packages, 142-143
  purchasing, 35
  sales, 179
Trade Show News Network, 100
trade shows, 100
transactions, canceling, 88
Turbo Lister, 101

U

UltraShip postal scales, 159
unclaimed PayPal payments, 16
unique listing identifiers, 53-54
unprofitable products, 183-184
unshipped items, 42
unsold items
  relisting, 55-56
  selling, 80-82
upgrading, 7, 50-51
UPIs (Unpaid Item Disputes), 34
UPS, 138-143, 150-151
upselling, 176
User IDs, 5-7
usernames, 5-7

USPS (United States Postal Service)
  domestic shipping, 137-138
  eBay/USPS Priority Mail boxes, 144
  home pick-ups, 141-142
  insurance, 143
  international shipping, 163-165
  Media Mail, 149
  pre-paid postage, 141-142
  shipping rates, 157-158
  tracking, 142-143

V-W-X-Y-Z

vacations, 113-114
verified PayPal accounts, 14
video clips, 99-100

watermarking photographs, 134
websites, linking in listings, 96-97
Western Union, 109
WhatDoISell?® (Seller Central), 83, 103, 195
white balance (photographs), 133
wholesalers, 186-189, 192-193
withdrawals, PayPal accounts, 15
Word, 48
Worldwide Brands's IMR (Instant Market Research), 102
writing descriptions, 46-49
writings, selling, 116

yard sales, as product sources, 185